## TURN HIM ON WITH THE SENSUALITY OF YOUR VIRTUOSO LOVEMAKING . . .

Produce the highest pitch of pleasure for your man with a sizzling round of fun and games. Show him the dark side of your scandalous, outrageous, unchaste sexual appetite. Become his tasty dish and make him hungry for more and more.

Be a one-woman sexual extravaganza—make him think you enjoy sex *too* much. Be his most passionate partner—his greatest lover.

Be an erotic artist.

Be a delight.

Be sensational. . . .

## HOW TO DRIVE YOUR MAN WILD IN BED

## SIGNET Books of Special Interest

# HOW TO DRIVE YOUR MAN WILD IN BED

by
Graham Masterton

A SIGNET BOOK
NEW AMERICAN LIBRARY
TIMES MIRROR

*For Wiescka*

COPYRIGHT © 1975 BY GRAHAM MASTERTON

SIGNET, SIGNET CLASSICS, MENTOR, PLUME AND MERIDIAN BOOKS
are published by The New American Library, Inc.,
1301 Avenue of the Americas, New York, New York 10019

FIRST PRINTING, JANUARY, 1976

1 2 3 4 5 6 7 8 9

PRINTED IN THE UNITED STATES OF AMERICA

# Contents

# *Introduction*

How can a man—any man—tell a woman how to drive a man wild in bed?

The answer is: better than any other woman. Because even if she's been the admired, adored, and arousing partner of a hundred men, a woman will never quite know what it is that makes her so attractive.

She could guess that it's her figure. But love is not born of breasts and bottoms alone.

She could guess that it's her face, her smile, her bubbling sense of humor. But often it's much, much more than these. It's an extra ingredient that even women who have it, and *know* they have it, find hard to put their finger on.

It's something that men will risk careers, marriages, and financial disaster to get. And it's something that you—whether you're a mistress already, whether you're planning to be a mistress, or whether you're a wife who wants to act like a mistress—could have for yourself.

But even though this extra ingredient is so hard to pin down, there is no secret about how you can acquire it—through hard work. If you're bothered by the idea of making an effort to raise yourself to the level of being a perfect lover, then you ought to stop reading now. Nothing that is worth having comes easily, and that goes double for sex.

This book is a course in erotic self-improvement. It tells you how sexual technique, exercise, diet, psychology, and understanding can build the sex life you already have and enjoy into something even more stimulating and successful. It is based on my personal experience as a man and a lover; on my ten-year editorship of some of the world's leading sex magazines, such as *Forum, Penthouse, Mayfair* and the Swedish porno magazine *Private;* and on the advice and assistance I have received throughout those years from psychiatrists, sexologists, sociologists, and even prostitutes.

What *is* a perfect playmate? Can such an exotic creature exist?

My definition of such a woman—and that extra something that makes her what she is—is this: *a perfect partner is a woman who gives better than she gets.* She is a woman who is sexually and socially creative enough to make a man feel that whatever he has given up for her—and whatever he gives to her—is more than worth it.

Women like this can and do exist, but they've always been a rare breed. They're rare because girls are hardly ever told, as they grow from girlhood into womanhood, what men are going to expect of them. They get a little sex education, yes. They're told about menstruation and conception and the arts and crafts of motherhood. Their mothers may even warn them about men who want more than a good-night kiss.

But most girls enter sexual relationships, and eventually marriage, with only the haziest notion of what they are capable of sexually, what they should expect from their sex lives, and how to make the most of themselves. They only have the vaguest idea of how sex should fit into their social encounters.

I've known women of nearly 30—sophisticated in every other way—who still think that you can't get pregnant the first time you make love, who have never heard of oral sex, and who basically haven't a clue about the way in which their own sex organs function, let alone those of a man.

And even those who have picked up the fundamental facts of life are very unsure of what to do when they're faced with a real live man in bed:

• Are you sure, for instance, that you know how to grip a man's penis to give him maximum erotic excitement?

• Are you sure you know how to fellate him properly?

• If he can't keep up his erection, are you sure it's not your fault—and what can you do about it, anyway?

• Are you sure you can help him to satisfy you and give you the orgasm you're dying to have?

• Do you know what sexual games turn him on—and those that definitely turn him off?

• After it's all over—do you know what to say?

Don't worry if you don't know the answers to all these questions—surprisingly few women do. They have a *rough* idea—they come up with some sort of answer—but then they hesitate and ponder and realize that maybe they're not so sure after all . . .

In these days of increasing female independence, why should any woman *want* to be a perfect lover? Doesn't that mean she has to spend her time being a slave to male sexual lust?

The point is this: every woman has enormous potential for enjoying herself in bed. In fact, as far as physical sensation goes, women are capable of having *more* fun with sex than men. Long after a man's cock has subsided with exhaustion, a woman can go on and on having satisfying and arousing climaxes.

This pleasure potential is within you now. You have a right to enjoy it. By training to be the perfect lover, all that erotic enjoyment is yours for the asking, and you'll be far from a slave to the man you're sleeping with. In fact, the better and more demanding you are, the better he'll have to be to keep up with you. You'll be the one with the edge on him—not the other way around.

*The Sensuous Woman* was all right in its way, but it never came to terms with the male sexual mentality. Inside a man's mind, all kinds of erotic fantasies are going on, just as they are in yours. But unlike most of yours, a man's sexual imaginings are almost always crude, vulgar, and *impersonal*. Most men don't think about having sex with Brigitte Bardot or Sophia Loren in the way you think about having it with Robert Redford or Paul Newman—they think about breasts and vaginas and weird variations.

One man I know recently got up the courage to tell his wife his innermost sexual thoughts. "I told her how I thought about twelve-year-old girls having intercourse with dogs. She wouldn't speak to me for a week, and wouldn't let me touch her for a month."

You can try asking your man or men what really goes on in that deepest corner of their minds where erotic fantasy lurks. But I don't guarantee you'll get an honest answer. All you have to do is realize that men *do* think this way, and that if you're going to drive your man wild in bed, you'll have to do things that cater to his fantasies.

That doesn't mean you have to go to bed with Rin Tin Tin, but it might mean that you find yourself wearing open-crotch panties, shaving off your pubic hair, or being tied hand and foot to the bed while he has his way with you.

Although you can't expect him to turn into Steve McQueen overnight, there are ways of coaxing a man into playing out *your* fantasies in return, and if you feel like being the Queen of Sheba one night, with your lover standing stark naked beside you feeding you diet chocolate, then that can be arranged.

The way I see it, the perfect mistress can expect to get as much potential out of her sexual activities as her lover.

This book will help you to achieve three things:

● First, it will assist you in understanding your own erotic potential, and how you can exploit it.
● Second, it will tell you what a man wants most from you in bed, and how to give it to him.
● Third, it will tell you how to get—and keep—the man you want.

That last point, to me, is extremely important. So many sexual textbooks assume right from the beginning that you already have someone waiting in your bed, without understanding that finding the bedmate you want can be the most difficult part of the whole sexual exercise. I'm not going to duck the issue.

I hope, too, that you're not going to duck out of the hard work that this training course requires. There are diets and exercises in it that need sticking to, if they're going to be of genuine help. There are sexual techniques that need practice and skill (and sometimes pain) to acquire, and you mustn't give up after the first try if it doesn't work out immediately. A good sex life isn't something that you're born with, any more than you're born with the ability to cook, or crochet, or take shorthand, or (I must appease the women's lib movement here) invent the hydrogen bomb. Why, out of all human activities, should sex be the only one in which training and counseling isn't considered essential—even though it is physically and psychologically complex, and affects our whole well-being?

It's not enough to know the facts. That's like describing a hammer and chisel and a piece of oak to a would-be carpenter, and then telling him to get on with it. What every woman needs is training that will not only equip her with the information, but also give her the means and the understanding to use it.

Your course in being a perfect lover starts here. Even though much of it requires application and effort, you won't find it unpleasant. (What course that tells you the best way of getting a man's penis to stimulate your clitoris could be?) I hope you enjoy it, and that when you're through, you'll know all the delights that a woman is entitled to . . . when she knows how to drive a man wild in bed.

GRAHAM MASTERTON
London, 1975

# 1.

## Well—Are You Any Good in Bed?

After you've made love, and you're lying there listening to your lover snoring away like a Bach organ recital, do you ever wonder what he really thinks of you as a bedmate?

Do you sometimes think that he might have lost interest in you a long time ago, and is now having sex with you simply out of habit?

Do you really turn him on? Do you play erotic games together? Or does he just put his leg over, bounce you up and down until you both reach a rather feeble climax, then turn over and go to sleep?

When was the last time you really did something *different*—something shocking, or surprising, or even vaguely dirty?

*Are you really any good in bed?*

The trouble is, it has always been difficult for women to get a clear idea of what "good in bed" actually *means* to men.

It's not that you don't talk about your personal sexual experiences with your friends—women do it more, and much more frankly, than most men would ever dare. It's just that there is much less explicit sexual reading available to women, and a good deal less straightforward erotic education.

Most sexy novels are written by men, so it's easy for a man to identify with the hero and compare his own performance with that of the fictitious stud. But what's a woman supposed to learn from passages like, "As he possessed her, she felt a wonderful warmth spread right through her body, and her mind felt full of stars"?

How is one warmth more wonderful than any other warmth? How do you get stars in your mind? It's romantic, and it's amusing, but it's of no practical help. And—let me say this at once—even though I believe in romantic love, I don't believe that romantic love can survive and flourish unless both you and your lover know the bald and practical *facts* of what you're doing. Yehudi Menuhin plays the violin very romantically, but what would he sound like if he hadn't bothered to learn the technical details of how to play?

Magazines such as *Cosmopolitan* and *Viva* tend to carry fairly specific articles about sex and sex behavior these days, but very few of them are straightforward "how-to" explanations. They contain nothing like the workmanlike information a man can pick up from reading *Playboy* or *Forum,* or from scrutinizing the full-color closeups of sexual organs that pornographic magazines provide.

So, as far as deciding whether you're good in bed or not, you're at a decided disadvantage. Another disadvantage is that your lover may not actually *tell* you if you're disappointing him.

This is Emma, a 26-year-old housewife, who recently broke up with her husband, Jim, a 30-year-old accountant:

"I'd always thought that our sex life was pretty good. When I married Jim, I'd slept with two other men, but I didn't know very much about sex at all, and I hadn't really had a close look at a man's penis or anything. Jim really taught me everything I know, and that's why in a lot of ways I blame him for what happened.

"We used to have intercourse two or three times a week, or whenever he felt like it. Obviously it didn't excite us as much after four years of marriage as it used to when we were first going out, but I don't think there was anything *wrong* with it—not that I could see, anyway. Jim used to turn me on, and then we'd have intercourse, and he'd bring me to a climax, and that would be it.

"When I found out he was having an affair with his secretary, I was absolutely shattered. I kept thinking to myself, Why, why, why? He likes living with me, he likes the person I am, he likes the way I cook, the way I bring up his child. He seems to like me in bed—at least he's never complained. I couldn't understand it, and not being able to understand it made it worse.

"In the end, he told me that he just didn't find me physically attractive any more. He found me dull in bed. I said I'd learn to do other things, I'd do *anything*, but he said it was too late. And that was that. I never really did find out what was supposed to be so wrong with me, and now I'm worried about having affairs with other men in case it all goes wrong in exactly the same way, because I'm no good in bed."

Emma's first mistake is to assume that, just because *Jim* doesn't think she's attractive and just because *Jim* finds her dull, that she *is* like that. From what she says, it's obvious that he wasn't exactly being the most exciting lover of all time, and that a great deal of the blame for what happened must rest on his shoulders. All the same, Emma did allow a tedious sexual routine to develop between them, and she expected Jim to take the initiative all the time in bed.

To that extent, she wasn't very good. But that didn't mean for a moment that she was hopeless. She was eager to learn, and if she'd understood what was happening sooner, she wouldn't have lost her husband.

But just because a woman knows lots of erotic tricks, and is passionate and enthusiastic, she isn't necessarily good in bed. Veronica, 28, nearly broke up with her boyfriend, 32-year-old Paul, because of her sexual behavior.

"It took him a long time to explain it to me, because he didn't want to hurt my feelings. I *was* a little hurt when he told me, but now I'm glad he did. I certainly think it's made things better.

"My trouble was that I always did the right thing at

the wrong time. Paul would come home in the evening feeling exhausted after the long drive home, and I'd look into his eyes and start smoldering, then open up his pants and take his cock out and start sucking it. But of course he wasn't really in the mood for that just then. It would be all right once a week, say, but not every night.

"Then there was something I used to do when we nearly reached a climax. I used to push my finger up his ass. That was all right sometimes, when we were a bit drunk or something like that, but my nails are quite sharp and he told me later that it used to throw him off.

"There were lots of other things like that. What it amounted to was that I was trying to do lots of little sexy things for him without thinking of how and when I should do them. That's why sex always seemed so clumsy and amateurish to him. I was horrified when he told me I was amateurish in bed, but now I understand what he meant."

Then there are hundreds of things that women just *can't* know—in the same way that men really *can't* know what it's like to feel a penis sliding into a vagina. But even though you may not be able to experience the actual sensation, a clear description can give you a pretty good idea of the effect you're having on the man you love.

Until you have some inkling of what it feels like to a man when you touch him in certain ways, when you grip his penis, or when you slip his balls into your mouth, then you will always find it difficult to assess how good you're being in bed.

And you're not just going to be good, you're going to be *perfect*.

Before you start improving your sexuality, it's worth finding out just how good—or bad—you are. It's also useful to examine your attitudes toward sex and lovemaking, because they will affect whatever you do to improve yourself.

For that reason, I've prepared a questionnaire that will help you to work out your sex profile, arming you with the knowledge of what you can do, what you can't do, and what you're prepared to learn to do.

It's important that you answer these questions without too much pondering and forethought, and that you're as honest with yourself as possible.

1. I am always rather frightened at the prospect of going to bed with a new lover—YES/NO.
2. I love my lover's penis—YES/NO.
3. I am always satisfied by my lovemaking—YES/NO.
4. My lovemaking is never romantic enough—AGREE/DISAGREE.
5. I am not satisfied with my body—AGREE/DISAGREE.
6. I am sometimes worried that my lover's penis will not fit inside me—YES/NO.
7. I enjoy taking the initiative in bed—YES/NO.
8. Sometimes I wish my lover would do more exciting things—YES/NO.
9. I enjoy having my lover's penis in my mouth—YES/NO.
10. I would like to have larger breasts—YES/NO.
11. Quite often I don't reach a climax—AGREE/DISAGREE.
12. I am quite confident that I know my lover's most sensitive spots—YES/NO.
13. I would never swallow my lover's sperm—AGREE/DISAGREE.
14. I like to fantasize about being raped—YES/NO.
15. I have very strong sexual fantasies—YES/NO.
16. Sometimes I think that unless I have a man, I'll go mad—YES/NO.
17. If my lover tried to have anal intercourse with me, I would resist—YES/NO.
18. I think men are very animal when they are having sex—YES/NO.
19. I don't like my lover looking closely at my vagina—AGREE/DISAGREE.

20. I enjoy having my vagina licked by my lover—YES/NO.
21. I would like to make love in front of a group—YES/NO.
22. I like a man to be sexually dominant—YES/NO.
23. I like the idea of having two men at once—AGREE/DISAGREE.
24. I am usually faithful to one man at a time—YES/NO.

Give yourself one point for each of the following answers: 1, no; 2, yes; 3, no; 4, agree; 5, agree; 6, no; 7, yes; 8, yes; 9, yes; 10, yes; 11, disagree; 12, no; 13, disagree; 14, yes; 15, yes; 16, yes; 17, no; 18, no; 19, disagree; 20, yes; 21, yes; 22, no; 23, agree; 24, no.

If you scored around 12, then you are a normal, sexually-interested woman who is anxious to improve her sexual technique and her abilities. If you scored more, then you have more than the makings of a sensuous woman. But don't worry too much if you scored less—that probably means that you're already well satisfied with your sex life, and if you are, then that's something to be pleased about.

A fairly average score (10–15) indicates that you harbor several uncertainties about the present state of your love life, particularly in terms of your own self-confidence and adventurousness. You're not too sure about your technique and how it's working on your lover, and it's possible that you're not entirely clear about all the physical details of sex, but you are plainly enthusiastic about widening the scope of your erotic experience.

A higher score shows that you are deeply sexually aware but dissatisfied with what you have now. You are prepared to do almost anything to broaden your sexual experience, and you have a highly liberated and balanced attitude toward the female role in lovemaking. You want to taste everything, and you're frustrated because you haven't. You're pretty good in bed now, but you could be terrific.

Because young girls tend to follow the example of

their lovers when they first have sex, it is often male ignorance and lack of sexual understanding that affects how a woman is going to perform in bed for the rest of her erotic life. All the same, sexual intercourse is like dancing: while the woman may depend on the man's lead, she still has to know where to put her feet, and both partners have to be equally creative to make what they're doing into something more than a mundane experience. You can't always blame the man and his clumsiness—particularly when it's in your power to do something to help him.

"We always made love in the same position," said 23-year-old Michelle. "He always climbed on top of me, and I always lay underneath, and that's the way we did it every time. Then one day I thought, Well, I don't have to put up with it. And *I* climbed on top of *him*. We both enjoyed it, and he wasn't upset that I'd taken the initiative. He'd just gotten stuck in a rut, and he needed a jolt to get him out of it."

But not all women have Michelle's spark of rebellion. Sandra, 22, told me, "The first man I ever slept with, when I was 19, was nearly twice my age. He didn't expect me to do anything—as long as I lay there with my legs open it was all right. He hardly even kissed me or cuddled me. I sometimes wished he would, but I didn't really know any better. So when I had sex with Terry, the boy I'm dating now, naturally I just lay there and let him get on with it. This went on for two or three weeks, and then he lost his temper. He said, 'Can't you move just a little bit? Are you asleep or something?' I was so upset, I cried. In the end I began to understand what to do, but what frightens me is that I could have gone on for the rest of my life thinking this was the way to make love—just lie there and wait for it all to happen."

A doctor with long experience in dealing with sexual problems said, "Things are far better these days than they used to be, but I am often still appalled at the ignorance of many girls and women when it comes to important matters of sex. I'm not blaming them—I blame their parents and their teachers and the whole system that makes it difficult for a girl to obtain information about sex and how people make love."

The saddest letter ever received by *Forum* magazine was from a 50-year-old woman who had read in the previous issue about orgasms. This was the first she had ever heard about them. She was filled with bitterness that her whole active sex life had passed without her ever having reached one. She felt cheated beyond belief.

Today, it's not fundamental information that's so desperately lacking. Most girls know enough about sex at the age of 16 not to make the classic mistake of the young married couple of twenty years ago who attempted to have sex with the bridegroom's penis pushed against his bride's navel. But what *is* lacking is the discussion and practical training that can make a woman more than a half-baked expert on gynecology, more than an obliging girlfriend or a dutiful wife. What is lacking is the means by which a woman can assess her sexuality and do something positive about improving it.

What is lacking is the way to help women get and give more pleasure in bed.

"I always used to think that my first boyfriend and I were good in bed," said 21-year-old Janet. "Then I dated a boy who was older, and he just left my first boyfriend standing, and made me feel like an idiot. I was so bad and so clumsy and so ignorant with him, that I wouldn't go out with him again."

"I thought I was bad in bed," confessed 31-year-old Eloise. "I'm one of those people who can't do anything rhythmical. I can't even tap my feet in time to music. But then I had an affair with a man who said I was absolutely marvelous. He said he'd never known anything like it. It bolstered my ego a bit, of course, but I think I know what I can do and what I can't. I mainly felt sorry for all those girls this man had slept with before, because if I'm bad, they must have been dreadful."

Helen, 25, said, "I used to think it wasn't very important, whether a person was good in bed or not. I used to enjoy sex, but it certainly wasn't the most vital thing in my life. I don't think I paid very much attention to it. Then one day my boyfriend and I had an awful argument, and as he stormed out, the last thing he shouted at me was, 'And another thing—you're a rotten fuck!' That was the most hurtful thing anybody had ever said to me. I suddenly realized that it *did* matter, if I was going to find the man I wanted and keep him. The only trouble was, I didn't know exactly what I was supposed to do about it."

Very few girls are so hopeless that they can't improve their sex lives. Very few girls are so *good* in bed that they can't improve themselves either. But one of the first things you have to realize is that you can't be expected to become a perfect lover on your own, without help. You need the help of a book like this, and you also need the help of an understanding lover. A man you can practice on. (If you don't have one right now, there are plenty of hints for finding one in a later chapter.)

The way you learn to communicate sexually with men is one of the most vital talents you can acquire. You can see how important it is from the women I have just quoted. In each case, a man and a woman got together, performed together the most intimate of physical acts, and yet still didn't really speak to each other about it. Do you stay silent when you dance with the man you love? Even when he steps on your toes, or you step on his? Then why don't you say something when you or he happens to make love clumsily—an act that is far more central to your happiness and emotional stability than the tango?

It is not unforgivable to be bad in bed. Casanova was often terrible in bed, and so was Catherine the Great. But it is unforgivable to sleep with someone time after time and never *tell* him or her they're bad in bed, and what they could possibly do about it.

I know why you don't want to tell your lover he's not very good in bed. Because you're scared you'll hurt his feelings, or he'll lose his temper, or your relationship will come to a highly abrupt end. But haven't you ever thought that, for the exact same reason, he may not be telling *you* that you're not very hot when it comes to sex?

The only way to get over an impasse like that is to do it together. That's why this book is designed to encourage you to concentrate on *practice* rather than *theory*. When it comes to sex, practice is much more fun than theory, anyway.

You now have a rough idea of how good you are in bed, and what kind of skills and insights you're going to have to acquire to improve yourself even more. And now's the time to take stock of your number-one sexual asset, and see just what you can do with that. . . .

# 2.

## *Your Vagina—Pleasure Your Greatest Treasure*

"There's a thing that bears a well-known name,
    Though it is but a little spot;
Its smell sets my heart and my brain aflame,
    And its touch makes my prick grow hot.
        'Tis the sweetest thing this world can show,
    To praise it can't be wrong;
'Twill set your blood in a fervid glow,
    Make your prick grow stiff and long.
'Tis a woman's cunt. Her glorious fan,
Oh, a cunt is the pride of an Englishman."

*The Pearl*, 1879

Between your legs you possess one of the most fascinating of all human organs, the vagina. As somebody once remarked, it's the original tunnel of love.

The vagina is much bigger inside than many girls—particularly young girls—appreciate. It is not just a tiny crack that could be split apart by a man's bludgeoning erection. In fact, sex doctors sometimes encourage girls to put their fingers inside to feel how elastic, capacious, and well lined the vaginal passages are.

The rings of muscle which make up the vaginal walls—and which give you the capability to grip your lover's cock when he enters you—are unromantically called the vaginal "barrel." But that's the best description there is. Your vagina is exactly like a barrel, hooped with muscle, and that muscle is absolutely crucial to the way in which you please your man.

When you're young and virginal, the muscles are tight, taut, and resilient. But as you grow older—and particularly if you've had any children—they grow slacker and less elastic. There's a male expression which describes making love to a woman with a loose vagina as "throwing a banana up Broadway." Naturally enough, because these muscles stimulate his penis when he makes love to you, a man prefers a tighter vagina.

There are several very simple ways in which you can keep your vagina in trim.

Exercise One: Wherever you are, whatever you're doing, contract your vaginal muscles for at least half an hour each day. The more you do it, the easier you'll find it is to control them, and soon you'll be able to develop a sassy little twitch which will be more than appreciated by your lover of the day.

Once your muscles are back in some sort of shape, it's time to start practicing on solid objects. Surprisingly enough, the best object to practice on *isn't* a real live penis, unless you can persuade your lover to hold still for fifteen minutes while you do your internal gymnastics. I can't, offhand, think of a single man who could stay motionless during that kind of treatment.

So acquire yourself either a dildo (artificial penis), a plastic vibrator, or a candle that is roughly the size of a male cock (about six inches long and one and a half inches in diameter). Insert your inanimate friend into your vagina, and then with your muscles alone, *squeeze* it right out of you. Go on repeating this exercise until you can send it shooting out like a bullet.

You'd be amazed, actually, how powerful the vaginal muscles can be once they've been trained. Honeysuckle Divine, the girl whose "Diary of a Dirty Broad" won her a certain dubious fame after its appearance in the New York sex newspaper *Screw,* has exercised her vagina to the point where she can take air in and out of it and blow a rudimentary version of "Yankee Doodle"; she can also squirt a popular brand of hand lotion to a distance of thirty feet. In a nightclub in Hamburg, striptease artists make a fortune in tips by doing full splits over coins that eager patrons throw onto the stage; they retrieve the coins by gripping them in their vaginas. Then there was the notorious English lecher who allowed a whore to keep all the gold pieces she could walk out of the room with in her vagina. It is reliably reported that she waddled out with twenty-four.

No one expects you to develop your vaginal abilities to the point of turning yourself into a circus act. To be great in bed, you don't have to be able to juggle plates with your vagina and have it accompany your lovemaking with a hummed version of "Abide with Me." But do appreciate that when you're actually having intercourse, those few square inches of soft and tender membrane inside your vagina are the most exciting area of contact with the man you love, and that means you have to use that tiny area to the utmost. With the vagina, you can caress him, stimulate him, excite him, control him, and eventually bring him to a climax. That's why it's so important that you work on getting the vaginal muscles into condition, and learn to operate them as sensitively as possible.

A man feels different sensations in his penis according to how deeply inside you he has thrust himself. At the entrance to your vagina, he feels a "ridgy" sensation, which is when the sensitive end of his penis, the glans, bumps its way past the inner lips, or labia minora, which during sexual excitement have become swollen with blood. If you like, imagine the labia minora when aroused as a kind of inflatable collar around the opening to your vagina.

As he plunges deeper, he feels a soft, wet, warm, and clinging sensation on the whole length of his penis. If you're in the right kind of position (legs over his shoulders, for example) he may even feel the neck of your womb, or cervix, with the tip of his cock. *You'll* certainly feel it—it's a very sensitive spot.

When you flex your vaginal muscles, he will feel on his penis a sensation rather like the sexual equivalent of going over a hump-backed hill in a car.

Your lover will derive full stimulation from your lovemaking through a combination of all these senations: the swollen labia minora, the moist vaginal interior, and the extra titillation you give him with your muscles. These same muscles contract and ripple fiercely when you reach a climax, which makes your orgasm almost as pleasurable for him as it is for you.

Women have asked me time and time again: What actually happens when I *come*? Do I shoot something out, like a man's ejaculation, when I reach a climax?

The myth of female "spending", as Victorian pornographers used to call it, has persisted for centuries. But in fact, you do not spurt any liquid out when you climax. The walls of your vagina, when you become sexually aroused, secrete a liquid lubricant, and continue to secrete it during intercourse. By the time you are intensely excited and reach orgasm, it is flowing quite freely, and that juiciness makes many women believe that they have just ejaculated like a man.

Incidentally, every woman has some flow of lubricant almost all the time, although the amount varies from day to day and at different times of the month. It has a very distinctive smell to it, which is nothing to worry about—in fact, you should worry if it *doesn't* smell, because the purpose of the odor is to arouse men. Although some women find it hard to believe, there are few things that turn on a man more than smelling the smell of freshly lubricated vagina. You would be doing yourself a sexual disfavor by using vaginal deodorants, as well as possible harm, since some of these chemicals can irritate sensitive vaginal tissues.

Mind you, I do stress that this smell is only attractive when *fresh*. It's the failure of some women to keep their vaginas clean that has led to the whole unpleasant male mythology of women smelling like fish. ("Evening, ladies," said the blind man, as he passed the fish store.)

Vaginal secretions are either clear or slightly milky. If they're anything else, you should check with your doctor. If you don't have *enough* lubricant for comfortable lovemaking, then ask your doctor for a hormone cream to stimulate the flow.

According to what position you're lying in, your vagina exerts different pressures on your lover's penis. It's worth finding out just what these pressures are, and you can do this easily with the aid of your dildo, vibrator, or candle.

Exercise Two: Lie flat on your back, naked, on your bed, and insert the vibrator into your vagina. Raise your legs in the air and feel where the vibrator rubs most if you push it gently in and out of you. Then turn on your side and repeat the exercise. Finally roll over on your stomach and try it like that. Also try it with your bottom raised in the air. In each of those positions, you should be able to detect that different parts of the vibrator—sometimes the tip, sometimes the shaft—are subjected to more friction and pressure than others.

Bear these positions in mind when you next make love. By knowing *what part* of a man's penis you are stimulating the most, you will know *how much* you are exciting him, since some parts are obviously more sensitive than others. In other words, you will be able to control the sexual feelings in his cock, and help to time them with your own sensations.

The idea of a woman controlling not only the timing of her own orgasm but that of her lover as well is something that doesn't often occur to most people. Many women assume that men go around "giving" orgasms, like boxes of after-dinner mints done up in pink ribbon. But it is *your* orgasm, it happens within *your* body, and your vagina is capable of bringing it on. What's more, by clever flexing of the muscles and subtle changes in the position of your legs, you can use your vagina to bring a man to a climax as well.

Why is this so important? For several reasons.

It's important for you to stop thinking that every sexual sensation you have within your vagina depends on what a man decides to do to you. Your pleasure and his pleasure will both be intensified by your stimulating vaginal actions, and he will come to understand more clearly that you are not just a passive object he has decided to take to bed, but a sexual being with demands and feelings and lusts of your own. You can never hope to be a perfect lover, until you can get this through your man's skull, because only then will he really begin to appreciate your erotic talents and join with you in the effort to make lovemaking better and better. A lot of men are sexually lazy. Many of them would prefer to have intercourse with life-size dolls which look and feel exactly like women, but just lie there silently until it is all over, and then go back into a closet until they are wanted again. This laziness will be perpetuated if you insist on behaving like one of those dolls. But if you challenge a man by being aggressive and sexy and stimulating, he will rise to the challenge (in more ways than one) and begin to exert himself. Part of the way in which you can make that challenge is through what you do to him with your vagina. That, to my mind, is *real* vaginal politics.

Little girls may possibly envy the penis dangling between their brother's legs, but even though the vagina is almost invisible, it is as versatile and arousing as a cock. It is a mistake to think of it as a hole, or a cavity. It's a tube, or a sheath, with active abilities of its own. It would probably help some men to start thinking of it like that, too.

What can you safely insert into the vagina apart from a penis? There are many things that a woman can do, and may be expected to do that involve pushing other things inside her. The only real restriction must come from common sense, however.

A London girl was recently taken to the hospital after masturbating with a test tube in her school chemistry laboratory. She sat down with it inside her and it broke, lacerating her vaginal walls. So one rule is not to use anything that might be breakable.

But anything smooth and phallic in shape will do. One woman wrote to me at *Penthouse* and said she liked to use a cucumber carved into the shape of a penis, and then slice it up later in the evening and serve it to her husband. When I was in Sweden, an amused husband wrote and told me about the way his wife masturbated with warm hard-boiled eggs at the breakfast table.

Don't insert anything that might harbor germs, or you will find yourself with a vaginal infection before you can say "bacteria." Don't insert anything electrical that is connected to the main supply. Don't insert empty soft drink bottles without caps on, because an in-and-out masturbating movement can cause strong suction to develop, and you may find the bottle impossible to remove. One well-known doctor told me that he was called to a woman's public lavatory after the attendant had heard screams of pain from one of the cubicles. It turned out that a woman had been masturbating with a Coke bottle, and that every time she tried to pull it out, it tugged at her womb, causing her intense pain. The doctor had to break the end of the bottle to release the vacuum.

While we're talking about it, don't ever insert anything into your urethra—the little hole that you pee from. In one hospital, there is a huge collection of objects that surgeons have removed from the bladders of women who have been turning themselves on in this way. The collection includes bobby pins, pens, clothes pins, and you name it. Apart from the obvious danger of "losing" the object, there is a very real danger of infection. Cystitis, as you no doubt know, is not the world's most desirable condition.

Even though I had hoped that the argument had died down years ago, I'm still asked by women who have vaguely heard of the controversy, and who are worried about its meaning and implication, what the difference is between a *vaginal* and a *clitoral* orgasm. Some time ago, sexologists became involved in a lengthy discussion on whether there were, in fact, two kinds of female climax. The clitoral climax was supposed to be an *immature* orgasm brought about by simple stimulation of the clitoris. The vaginal climax was supposed to be deeper and more mature and womanly.

The whole argument was a lengthy and confusing waste of time. It is clear now that women have only one kind of climax—even though different climaxes, brought about in different ways, can feel different. And, despite all the things you're learning to do with your vaginal muscles, this climax is brought about by one thing only—the arousal of the clitoris.

# 3.

# *The Seat of Sensation*

When discussing sexual organs, there always comes a point when words are not really enough. You have to ask people to take off their clothes, stand in front of the mirror, and examine themselves in detail. And if you're not reading this on the bus, that's what I'd like you to do now.

Open your legs and part the outer lips of your vulva as far as you can. The word vulva, by the way, simply means those parts of your sex organs that are normally visible. At the lower end of your outer lips, you'll see the vaginal entrance, which we've just been talking about, and the labia minora, the internal lips which swell with blood when they're aroused. Just above the vagina, too, you'll be able to see the small urethral opening, into which we do not stick ballpoint pens.

Above the urethra, under a little hood formed by the meeting of the inner lips, is a pea-shaped protrusion, and this is the clitoris. You may have a large clitoris or you may have a small one, but you do have a clitoris. I say that because many women (and men) are not quite sure where it is, and have trouble finding it.

The clitoris is the female equivalent of the male penis, and like the penis, its tissues become engorged with blood when you are aroused, and it stiffens. The little pea you see is in fact only a small part of the whole organ, which is concealed inside you. It is the stimulation of the clitoris that physically turns you on, and the excitement of everything that happens around your sex organs during intercourse is caused by the direct or indirect way in which the skin around the clitoris is rubbed or tugged. Even the action of your lover's penis as it slides in and out of your vagina is principally pleasant because it pulls on the labia minora, and thus on the clitoris.

When sexologists in the 1950's discovered the importance of the clitoris in lovemaking, they all went berserk, suggesting complicated techniques of intercourse whereby the man was supposed to "bounce" his penis on the clitoris with every thrust. This was not only complicated and unnecessary, but was often painful as well. Usually, the pressure of the man's pubic bone against the clitoris is enough in the way of direct stimulation to bring you to a climax.

I'll bet a dime to a dollar that you know how to massage your own clitoris to bring yourself to orgasm. But does your lover know? And if he doesn't, how can you go about teaching him?

Listen to Francesca, 24, a fashion model and promotion hostess:

"Stanley wasn't sure, I don't think, where my clitoris

was. It doesn't surprise me, because it took me ages before *I* was sure. I used to rub myself there whenever I was feeling sexually frustrated, but I wasn't sure exactly where it was. You don't spend hours in front of the mirror examining yourself with your legs apart.

"Anyway, our sex life together grew worse and worse, because although I loved him, and I wanted to have sex with him, he just never turned me on enough. I wasn't really turned on yet when he put his prick in me, and by the time he'd managed to get me a little bit aroused by making love to me, he'd come, and that was it.

"In the end, I took his hand and held it between my legs, guiding his finger to the right spot. He missed it a few times, but after a while he began to get the hang of it, and it was beautiful. He brought me off just with his fingers the first time. Then he tried licking me out with his tongue, and that was the first time he actually saw my clitoris close up. Once he understood, things were fine."

But was Stanley embarrassed or upset at having his lack of knowledge revealed?

"A little, because I don't think any man likes to be shown or told things about sex by his girlfriend. He thinks he's supposed to know it all already. But I think the obvious pleasure he was giving me—well, that really made up for it."

You don't have to be quite as blunt as Francesca was, if you don't want to. It's usually enough to murmur, when his fingers reach the sensitive spot, "Mmm . . . right on my clitoris." If he doesn't get the message then, he may need a hearing aid.

There are all kinds of ways in which you—and your lover—can stimulate your clitoris. Apart from the normal stimulation that it receives during lovemaking, there are devices called, believe it or not, "clitoral stimulators," which a man can attach to his penis during sex to give you an added thrill. They're not all that expensive, and they look rather like a rubber ring with a miniature bathmat attached. As your lover thrusts his penis in, the little bathmat is supposed to rub against your clitoris and give you intensified erotic sensations. According to those women I've talked to who have tried them, they're not all that terrific, but you might find that you respond to them better than most.

Don't be afraid to rub your own clitoris during love-making if it helps to turn you on. You can usually only do this comfortably when the man has entered you from behind, and if you're lucky, he may do it for you. In fact, you should encourage him to do it for you. But if you just want to give yourself an extra sexual boost as your climax appears on the horizon, it's quite all right to rub yourself a little bit to bring on the final orgasm. A word of caution, though: Don't get into the *habit* of strongly stimulating your clitoris every time you make love, or you may find that you can't have an orgasm unless you do, which, like every other habitual technique that people find essential to achieve satisfactory sex, can be a nuisance.

It doesn't make any difference, erotically speaking, whether you have a large clitoris or a small clitoris. In some African countries, there used to be a ceremonial clitoredectomy performed on young girls, which involved the removal of the skin "hood" around the clitoris; this was supposed to make them more sexually sensitive. As far as I can gather, it made no physiological difference at all, and was extremely painful.

Having checked out the clitoris, it's time too see what amazing pleasures it can bring you. . . .

# 4.

## *There's the Rub*

Most women still haven't quite come to grips with the new *acceptability* of masturbation. Suddenly, it's okay to admit out loud that you played with yourself in your adolescent years, and even more okay to admit that you *still* do it. Masturbation for women is even being regarded as a *therapy* for certain sexual problems, and Masters and Johnson have used it with success to assist women who have trouble in reaching a climax.

Could this actually be the same masturbation that caused you such shame and embarrassment in your teen-age years? The frantic fantastic rubbing between your thighs, with one ear cocked in case your mother came in to say good night?

It certainly could be. And what's more, this same masturbation can help you to explore the responses of your own body, and tone yourself up for the joys and pleasures of being a perfect lover.

Says Linda Lovelace in her book *Inside Linda Lovelace*, published by Pinnacle, "I started diddling when I was eleven or twelve—when it started feeling good—and would cause all kinds of family trouble by lingering so long in the bathroom. Maybe I had discovered how good a Prell Shampoo bottle felt as I rubbed it between my cunt lips and against my clit. Another time it might be a bar of slippery soap that had turned me on. I was primarily an *object* diddler. There were times when I might resort to a fingertip, but not often. I liked external things to rub against me. Later, of course, I discovered the vibrator and have been something of a slave to it ever since.

"Besides regular sex, of which I get plenty, I would say I masturbate to orgasm at least fifty times a day."

Now, if you're leading a moderately normal life, you undoubtedly won't have the time to masturbate fifty times a day. But it's not your climax-count that's important—it's your *attitude* toward self-stimulation. If you can begin to see it as a perfectly harmless entertainment, you're taking a sizable step forward in your sexual progress. If you can then understand that over and above its entertainment value, masturbation is actually *beneficial*, you're well on your way to giving the kind of pleasure to yourself and the man you love that is usually reserved for winning $500,000 on the lottery.

Despite the fact that confident ladies on late-night TV talk shows bandy the word "masturbation" around with impressive ease, you may not feel quite the same assurance about it yourself. Don't worry—even in today's liberated climate, you're not alone. Even highly sophisticated lovers still admit that they feel a little reserved about admitting they masturbate, and even more reticent about doing it in front of someone else.

That's not surprising. It was only a few years ago that masturbation was regarded as "pollution," and "the solitary sin." It was rude. It was *playing with yourself*. Our parents were a little more tolerant toward it than *their* parents, who were schooled in matters of sex by such upright tracts as *What Every Young Woman Ought To Know*, in which 15-year-old girls were warned of the doomsday consequences of "the secret vice." But all the same, most of our parents didn't face up to the fact that masturbation is physically harmless, and is only emotionally damaging if you feel guilty about doing it.

You can masturbate yourself until you're blue in the face, but all that you will suffer will be an aching wrist. You will *not* become frigid or nymphomaniac or infertile. You certainly won't need to consider any of the bizarre and extreme "cures" for masturbation that nineteenth-century doctors believed were necessary—such as tying your hands together at night, or wearing a chastity belt, or even cauterizing the clitoris with a white-hot iron. In 1894, at a hospital in Ohio, a girl even had her clitoris *removed* for willful and persistent masturbation.

Almost every woman masturbates in one way or another at one time or another. It's nice, and it's a turn-on, but it can be more than that. It can be a way of preparing your sexual nerve-endings for some of the most thrilling sex you've ever had. Unless you masturbate, and *until* you masturbate, you won't know very much at all about your own sexual likes and dislikes, and the geography of your genital responses. You wouldn't try and win a pinball championship without knowing how a pinball machine worked, and in the same way you've got to discover the "tilt" and "score" mechanisms of your own sexual organs.

The writers of *Understanding Human Sexual Inadequacy,* a study of Masters and Johnson's newest work, published by Little, Brown & Co., expained that, "Although marriage manuals stress clitoral foreplay, very little has been said about how to do it and how much to do it." By watching women masturbate in the laboratory, Masters and Johnson noted a variety of clitoral manipulative techniques. *Actually, no two women among their subjects masturbated the same way.* Most often they stimulated the entire genital area, which causes a clitoral response regardless of whether that organ is directly touched. The result of overall manipulation is a slower arousal, but it leads to a fully satisfying climax, and it is less likely to be painful or irritating.

You see what they're saying. They're saying that no book in the world can explain how *your* genitals can be best aroused. Only *you* can discover that, and the only way to discover that is through masturbation. Unlike *The Sensuous Woman,* who suggests you draw the drapes from time to time and writhe about on your bed with your favorite hairbrush handle, I'm convinced that the simplest and most practical way to get the best out of masturbation is to do it *regularly* and *thoughtfully,* as part of a planned sexual training.

Don't get me wrong—I'm not trying to treat your sexual organs like stripped-down components of a Kawasaki motorcycle. Masturbation should be sexy and full of fantasy, as well as purposeful and progressive. But do try to understand *why* you're doing it, and what you can get out of it—and, above all, what it can teach you about having sex with the man you want.

First of all, take off your clothes—all of them. You should have done this already for chapter three, but I think I might forgive you if you do it now. Hold book in left hand. Lie back on bed or couch. Now part thighs and let fingers of right hand stray seductively between legs. Imagine they're your lover's fingers, and not your own. Imagine they're mine, if you like—I'm known for my very erotic fingertips.

Now place the tip of your index finger in that tiny dimple where your vaginal cleft begins, somewhere amid your pubic hair. Feel that tiny dimple? Caress it, and see what happens.

Work your finger gradually southwards, sliding it between your vaginal lips like a plow working a wet furrow. Feel the ridge of your clitoral shaft. Toy with it. Then hook your fingertip around underneath it as it stiffens, and rub it gently upwards. Probe the whole clitoral area for the spot that turns you on the most.

Slide even further down. Touch your urethra. Run your fingers around the opening of your vagina. Test every single nerve-ending, every square millimeter of sensitive flesh. Don't be shy of yourself. Your lover is going to be touching you here, and if you're not shy of *him,* then your own investigations shouldn't embarrass you. After all, you've known you all your life.

Don't stop at the vagina when you're palpating your erotic nerve-endings. Go lower, to the perineum, the sensitive bridge between cunt and anus. Some ladies like to have it delicately scratched with the tip of the fingernail. See if you do. And don't ignore your anus, which is packed with nerve-endings. Do you like a finger to go sliding up it, or does it hurt? Do you like having it pinched and tickled, or not?

The information you glean from this physical self-inspection may be old news to you, particularly if you've been masturbating since you came out of Mickey Mouse ears. But it's surprising how many seasoned self-stimulators have never bothered to analyze which kind of masturbation technique turns them on the most.

Here's Lynn, 29, talking about her own masturbation technique: "It took me a long time to find out just how I liked a man to touch me between my legs, because I always used to masturbate by pressing my thighs together, and kind of rubbing them around and around. An incredibly sexy sensation used to rise up between my legs. I pressed my thighs tighter and tighter until my climax seemed to pop open like a small flowerbud at the base of my spine, and then bloom up and up until my cunt started contracting and twitching, and that was *it*. I mean, I knew *how* to masturbate. I often did it five or six times a week, almost every time I went to bed. But I didn't know what it was, what particular sexual organs I was pressing between my thighs to give me those feelings.

"In the end, I found out almost by accident. I was shaving some of my pubic hair away from the sides of my thighs so that it wouldn't show when I wore a bikini. I had to hold the lips of my cunt together to get the razor in at the side, and I began to feel this really nice sensation. It was simply because I was holding my clitoris between my finger and my thumb, and gently rubbing the sides of it around and around. I liked to have my clitoris *squeezed* and *rotated*. I was quite excited that I knew just what it was that turned me on. I told my boyfriend, Carl, and he put his hand in my panties and did it to me. The feeling was even better. He worked me up in about fifteen seconds until the warm juice was actually sliding down my legs. I had a climax just like that, standing up in the kitchen."

And this is Lois, 23, talking about her own self-discovery: "I was brought up to believe that it was dirty and pretty disgusting to touch your own vagina. You were allowed to wash it, and you had to insert tampons in it, but beyond that the whole thing was tabu. It took me a long time to start to masturbate. I didn't do anything until I was 18 or 19, and then I used to jerk myself off when I came home after heavy dates with boys. I had to do it, because my panties used to be soaking. All I did then was put my hand between my legs and rub myself for five or ten minutes. I always felt guilty about it afterwards, but I used to think, Well, okay, but at least it's better than having sex with a boy you don't truly love.

"I found out about myself after an anatomy lesson at college. There was a diagram of the female sex organs in a book, and I was fascinated to see how they really looked. So when I got home, I locked my bedroom door and opened my legs in front of the mirror. I pulled my lips apart with my fingers and started touching myself and probing around. I found that if I stroked myself gently just below my clitoris, touching my urethra at the end of the stroke, then I had these amazing sensations that sent shivers all the way up me."

Remember that you may not always like to masturbate in quite the same way every time. Your technique will depend on your mood. So it's important for you to identify which technique goes with which mood, and be capable of explaining this to your lover.

For instance 17-year-old Emma told me, "Sometimes I feel in a very romantic mood, and I like to lie there on my bed and play romantic music and play with myself very gently, hardly touching myself. I like to brush my fingertips around my breasts and down my stomach and around my thighs, and then touch myself so carefully and softly between my legs. That kind of turn-on can last me for hours. Sometimes I come so quietly and easily that I hardly know it's happened. But other times I feel in a dirty mood, and I want to do something crude and rough. That's when I squat naked on the floor and push big white wax candles up my asshole, and I sometimes blow the hairdryer against my cunt and rub myself with the spout of it. I know it's crude, but that's what makes it so exciting. I'm not ashamed of it. I don't know what I'd do if Mother found out. I don't think she'd understand. But I don't see what harm it could do. It gives me such fantastic feelings, and if I didn't do it I think I'd go crazy from frustration."

Try as many different kinds of masturbation as you can. You may, unexpectedly, come across a technique that makes your spine melt and your teeth rattle. Some of the favorite masturbation techniques for women are these:

● Draw a furled silk scarf backwards and forwards between your legs so that it rubs against your vulva and clitoris.

● Lie back in the tub and play the shower against your vagina and clitoris, seeking out the most sensitive spots with the spray.

● Insert a phallus-shaped object (carve a cucumber into shape if you don't have a proper dildo) into your vagina, and keep it there all day, held in place by tight panties.

● Give your vulva a working-over with an electric vibrator, making a note of the exact places that give you the greatest thrill.

● Pour fresh whipped cream on your vulva and entice your pet cat into licking it off.

● Press your vulva against the corner of your washer/dryer when it's humming away at full throttle.

● Telephone your boyfriend, husband, or lover, and while he's talking to you, rub the receiver between the lips of your vulva. Tell him what you're doing if you like. He might be worried because you've suddenly started talking in squelches.

Don't hesitate to use sexy magazines or books to stimulate you while you masturbate. They can actually be helpful in discovering what turns you on most about men. If you find that the sight of a giant-size cock arouses you more than anything else, or that you're driven crazy by a well-muscled back, or that a guy in tight satin jeans turns you on, you're one step closer to understanding your own desires a little more, and thus one step closer to putting them into practice.

Very few men are put off by the idea of a woman who masturbates—even a woman who masturbates while looking at pictures of other men. This letter, which was sent to me when I worked for the Swedish porno magazine *Private*, is quite typical of male attitudes toward girls who turn themselves on.

"I had been out for a walk in the evening, and when I returned the light in the house was on. I went to the window and saw my lovely wife at a table reading a book. Standing there admiring her, I noticed that she suddenly moved her right hand from the table toward her lap.

"Slowly she put her hand under her skirt, in between her wonderful thighs. After a few seconds her hand and arm started to shake rhythmically, and only then did I realize that she was masturbating—an act that I had never had the fortune to watch during our marriage thus far. It was fantastic. She went on for a few minutes, then she pulled down her pants, legs apart, and exposed her lovely pussy for me which was slightly parted with her red clitoris clearly visible between the moist lips. She continued working her pussy and clitoris very hard. I then realized she had reached her climax. She pulled down her skirt and wiped her fingers between her thighs, as they were all wet with foam from her pussy. She smelled her fingers, kissed them, and went back to reading as if nothing had happened.

"Now and then my wife and I discuss sex in general, and especially masturbation, but my wife declares that she never masturbates—no, not her. She says she cannot understand what good women can get out of it. Wives can be funny, can't they?"

The important point about masturbation is not to see it as a *substitute* for intercourse. It never can be, and if you think of it like that, you will always regard it as second-best and something to be ashamed of. There may be times when you don't have a man, and you will masturbate to keep the sexual wolf from the door. That's okay. But the real purpose of masturbation in your sex life should be: (1) to give you erotic pleasure and entertainment; and (2) to help you discover more about your own sexual responses.

This is Tina, 22, describing how she changed her mind about masturbation: "I thought, to be honest, that it was something depraved. But one day, when I had my period, a boyfriend of mine whom I loved and trusted, masturbated me instead of making love to me. It was then that I worked the whole thing out in my mind. I thought to myself, What the hell is the difference between him doing it to me and *me* doing it to me? So one evening, I went home, and when I was taking my shower, I rubbed the cake of soap between my legs and turned myself on. I had a real orgasm, and I enjoyed it. I felt like I was liberated—truly liberated. I had the ability to give myself sexual excitement at my own fingertips. I masturbated almost all night that night— over and over again, enjoying every orgasm I had and everything about it. I still masturbate a lot. Sometimes I just sit there watching television, and I put my hand into my panties and work myself off. I've even done it in front of a boyfriend of mine, and he responded to it real well. He was amazed, and very turned on. He took his cock out and masturbated himself, and splashed his sperm on the carpet. I'm not ashamed to say that I masturbate. I love it. I'd do it anywhere, in front of anybody. I think it's more disgusting to be revolted by masturbation than it is to masturbate."

Maybe Tina's views are a little further out than yours. But do try and get yourself into a frame of mind that will allow you to turn yourself on without guilt or apprehension. Masturbation can only do you good, and the more you do it, the less of an anxiety-ridden Big Deal the whole idea of masturbation will become.

In fact, I have a great idea. Since you're naked right

now, why not masturbate yourself right up to an orgasm before you get into the next chapter? Fingers ready? Here you go . . .

# 5.

## *The Perfect Penis*

"I'll follow that man
With his old peg and awl."
—Old English Folk Song

Between the legs of men dangles this extraordinary and mysterious piece of equipment that's been surrounded with more myth and misunderstanding than almost any other part of the human body.

The penis—cock, prick, dick, dingus, wang, John Thomas, pecker, tool, willie, you name it.

Actually, the action and construction of the penis are far from difficult to understand, and even the subtler problems that affect it are not hard to grasp. Basically, it is nothing more than a sponge. Inside the shaft of the penis is a network of spongy tissue that fills up with blood when the man is sexually aroused. A restrictive valve prevents blood from leaving the penis at the rate at which it is entering, and therefore the shaft becomes swollen and hard. Hey, presto—erection.

The plumlike head of the penis, or gans (sometimes, because of its shape, called "the fireman's helmet"), is full of hypersensitive nerve-endings which respond to friction and rubbing. Probably the most sensitive single part of the whole organ is the frenum—a stringlike piece of skin which is located just behind the opening in the end of the penis.

The actual spermatozoa, the live male seed, are produced in the balls, or testicles, which hang in the pouch of skin called the scrotum. They dangle out there in the breeze because the production of sperm requires a temperature lower than that of normal body heat. The scrotum's wrinkles help to radiate heat away from the balls, and thus keep the temperature down. You may have noticed that when it's cold, a man's balls shrink and tighten, and this is because the scrotum is keeping *in* heat.

After they've been made by the testicles, the sperm proceed up a tube, where they're joined by white seminal fluid produced by the prostate gland. This fluid nourishes and protects the sperm, and keeping them alive during their forthcoming trip up the penis and into your vagina.

When the man's penis is stimulated enough, this fluid pours into the tube that runs up the middle of his cock, and the sensation that this produces starts off a spasmodic muscular reaction. The semen is spurted out in three or four jets, and if you weren't standing in the way, it could go as far as ten feet.

While a man is having an erection, the tube to his bladder is closed off, and so it is impossible for him to urinate during sex.

Despite the fact that Victorian pornographers described the penis as "a massive engine" and a "ramrod," it's worth knowing that a man's erection is a good deal frailer than erotic fiction suggests. If you're not careful, you could do or say something that would make your lover's "massive engine" shrivel up to the size of a child's balloon.

Men can be stimulated into having an erection by many things—pictures of naked women, reading a dirty book, watching a striptease, being fondled, thinking about going to bed with you, imagining sexy activities. A woman once asked me if having an erection *hurt*. The feeling varies, actually. Sometimes a man can have an almost involuntary erection that feels like nothing more than having a bone in his trousers, and sometimes, when he's more aroused, the whole penis can feel tingly and swollen and full of sexual anticipation.

Most men have some kind of erection first thing in the morning—a boon to the aged, and often called the "morning glory." This erection is primarily caused by pressure on the bladder, which is bursting to get rid of last night's drink intake, and shouldn't be counted on too much as evidence of erotic arousal.

Just as many things can get an erection up, so can many other things cause it to come down again. Alcohol, although it may make a man feel amorous, will almost certainly give him the condition known as "brewer's droop." Narcotics and tranquilizers do the same. Anxiety and tension are other causes of erection failure. If your lover can't rise to the occasion, he may be worried about: (1) making love to you; (2) what his wife is going to think; (3) his unpaid electricity bill; (4) anything at all.

Anxiety, in fact, is the main cause of temporary impotence, and it has a rather nasty way of spiraling. Because the man is anxious, he can't get an erection, and because he can't get an erection, he gets anxious, and so he can't get an erection. If you suspect that your lover is caught in this downward nosedive, then it will take all your tact and understanding to pull him out of it. Don't nag and criticize his inability to get a hard-on—that will only make matters three times worse. Don't even joke about it, because his virility is one subject that no man will ever find funny. Just keep on caressing him and stimulating him until you can get Fido to grow, and if he topples again, don't lose patience, start caressing him again. In the end, your tolerance will pay off, and you'll be able to feel as proud about it as he does.

If your lover is persistently unable to get an erection, even though you have no reason to believe that anything is wrong, he may need to visit a doctor. Don't encourage him to use sex aids, such as inflatable penis splints and other gadgets (yes, they really exist), because he may grow dependent on them without ever really solving his problem.

What if your lover has the opposite problem with his penis—he can get it up and get it in, but the minute he's there he ejaculates, and it's all over before you've had time to blink?

This condition is called premature ejaculation, or *ejaculatio praecox*, and it's sometimes triggered off by nerves. Try him again tomorrow, when he's not so all-fired excited by the prospect of screwing you, and you may find he's better. If he's not, get him to masturbate (or masturbate him yourself) about an hour before you plan to make love. Or get him to try a desensitizing spray (there are several available at most drugstores). He could also try wearing a condom, which might cut down his hair-trigger ejaculation by a few minutes.

Usually, premature ejaculation is a nervous habit, which can be stopped.

But if it persists, take a look at Chapter 11.

What size should your lover's penis be, and if it's really big, will you be able to get it inside you comfortably?

The average penis is about six inches long when erect. The world's longest known penis now is about fourteen inches, but it's unlikely that you'll encounter it, unless you happen to live in the East African bush, where it and its owner were last sighted.

As we've seen, your vagina is quite capable of accommodating a penis of average size, plus a couple of inches more. Even though your lover may look enormous when he's got a hard-on, you'll have no trouble fitting him in. The only possible problem you may have is *vaginismus*, which is the medical name for a violent contraction of the vaginal muscles. This is almost always caused by emotional upset, and this emotional upset is almost always caused by fear of being entered by so large an organ. If you find that *you* suffer from it, your friendly neighborhood doctor will soon be able to help you with tranquilizers.

When he reaches a climax, a man usually ejaculates about a teaspoonful of semen. Sometimes it's more, sometimes less, depending on when he last had sex, his health, and other factors. Don't think you can measure it out, though, and discover whether he's been unfaithful to you.

How soon after a climax can a man have another erection? Well, if your lover can stand it (some men's penises are too sensitive afterwards) you might find that by rubbing him *hard* immediately after making love once, you can turn him on enough to make love right away for a second time. Usually, though, he'll need anywhere from fifteen minutes to half an hour to recover. Not many men over the age of 25 can make love more than three or four times in a single night, and you might have to leave him alone the morning after.

Your attitude toward your lover's penis will count for a lot. Get to know it, because familiarity with what it can do (and what it can't do) will reward you in increased pleasure. Be admiring and friendly toward it, and your lover will appreciate that.

I can't say too often, though, that if you want to keep a man's respect and affection, you should never make fun of his limp penis. Joke about it when it's stiff, but never when it's dangly. I'm not personally sensitive about it, because I recognize that it would be more than tiresome to walk around all day with a permanent erection, but I know a great many men who are. I know some men who even lie face-down after they've made love because they don't want their girlfriends to see the funny little brown sausage lying so meek and helpless on the left thigh.

Talking of left thighs, it may help you when you're in the mood for groping your lover's penis through his jeans to know that most men "dress to the left." In other words, since a man can't walk around with his penis pointing straight out in front of him, he places it sideways, pointing left. So, if you care to examine the pants bulge of the man nearest you, you will note that the bulge on the right-hand side is a testicle (sensitive, and not for savage squeezing) while the bulge on the left is the object of your affection. The second testicle, if you're interested, is tucked further back, more between the legs. Fascinating, isn't it?

# 6.

## *Finding a Man to Drive Wild in Your Bed*

"She look'd in my face, and on our eyes catching,
I just turn'd my head to see what she was scratching;
She had got her right ankle upon her left knee,
Up to her left garter I fairly could see.

"And ten minutes after she did it again,
Though knowing I look'd and saw it quite plain;
Come—there was a prank for a delicate virgin,
Who thought an old bachelor wanted some urging!"

—"Temptation," anonymous, 1880

Why it should be considered unacceptable for a woman to go hunting for the man she wants, when men are quite entitled to pursue whatever woman takes their fancy, I shall never know. I realize that some women *prefer* to be chased and seduced by men, but there are countless situations when, for various reasons, the man needs to have the fact of your interest in him pushed under his nose. Or perhaps he requires a little bit of cajoling and maneuvering before he will appreciate how much he really wants you.

Men have an extrordinary lack of self-confidence when it comes to meeting and seducing girls. Apart from the dashing few who have diamond-hard egos and an unshakable belief in their own attractiveness to women, men are either shy, reticent, and tongue-tied, or over-boastful and leaning backwards to impress.

You have to make up your mind what you want *in* a man and *from* a man. Of course, if you want regular meals in expensive restaurants, rides in a luxurious car, and all the fur coats you can wear at once, then there are plenty of men with lots of money and no looks who will be more than happy to provide. I would never criticize a woman for gold-digging, because it's a fact of life: supply and demand. The man wants a beautiful woman on his arm and in his bed, and that's the price he has to pay for it.

But if you want a man who is reasonably handsome, has personality and integrity, and has some love to offer you, then you'll have to tread more carefully. In fact, you'll have to give to him as much as you want him to give to you. Sometimes more.

And supposing he's already married—or, at the very least, is already involved in a long-standing and happy affair with another woman? Then you have to have a great deal of strength, and you have to make a number of extremely hard, painful, and unpleasant decisions. If the man wants to have an affair with you, you will have to understand that he has other responsibilities which at any time may take absolute priority over you and your love for him. You can ask him to stay with you; you can ask him too leave his wife, his family, and his home—but you can never expect it as a right. I'm not talking about Christian morality here—I'm talking about the plain facts of human emotion. For many men, giving up their families for another woman is too high a price to pay.

That's not to say that I think for a moment that "the other woman" is in the wrong. Few men are naturally monogamous to the extent that they can be satisfied with one woman all their lives (just as few women can really be satisfied with one man). Affairs with married men happen for a *reason,* and that reason is usually to be found in the man's marriage. Something is lacking— whether it's his wife's fault, or his own, or both—and *your* arrival on the scene may seem like just the answer to his problems. What I'm saying is that you must enter an affair with a married man with your eyes open, prepared to enjoy the best but expect the worst.

If you're a career woman, the most likely place for you to find a man is in your office or in connection with your job. While it's often the subject of jokes and cartoons, the boss-secretary relationship is, in real life, one of the commonest. But if you're interested in your boss, how do you go about snaring him?

There's a thin line to tread between hyperefficiency and inefficiency. If you're too good a secretary, if you file everything perfectly, always arrive on time, and generally organize his office so that it runs without a hitch, it's unlikely that he'll want to become sexually involved with you. He values you too much to want to make a pass. If you refuse him and leave in a huff, what is he going to do without you? On the other hand, if your letters are full of mistakes, and there are grubby fingermarks all over your envelopes, and your filing cabinet looks like the town dump, he won't respect you at all, and there's very little chance that he will want to keep you around purely for erotic entertainment.

So be hard-working and reasonably efficient, but take days off now and again, and when it rains, arrive fifteen minutes late. Don't dress up too much: a man at work is embarrassed by skirts that are too short and too much exposure of breasts. His colleagues will start nudging him and winking and saying, "Your secretary's quite a piece, Bill," and he won't feel at all comfortable with you.

Seducing a boss is usually a fairly long-term exercise. That's because it takes time for him to adjust his view of you from someone he works with, and leaves behind at the office when he goes home, to a sexually attractive woman in your own right. Chat with him fairly frequently, and slowly build up a picture of you and your background and your personality in his mind, so that he gets familiar with you without even realizing it. This procedure will also give *you* the chance to get to know *him*.

Supposing you've carefully led your boss through all these preparatory stages, and he still doesn't bite? The invitation to drinks after work never comes, and he still doesn't look any more interested than he did before? *Don't give up.* What he needs is a push—something to make him realize that he does, after all, find you rather attractive.

Turn up in your prettiest dress one day and announce that it's your birthday (whether it is or not). Or come to him and say you have a problem that you need his help in unraveling, and invent some long and complex story about how your landlord is going to evict you for some misdemeanor you've never committed—a story so involved that it needs a quiet drink somewhere out of the office to discuss properly. Or failing either of these ploys, have a small party and invite him along.

The important thing is to get him out of the office and into a setting where he suddenly realizes that he's escorting an attractive woman. His normal masculine instincts will then automatically respond to you, and if you have any chance at all, you'll have it then. Try and avoid talking about work and the office, because his mind will start reverting to his "boss" role, and the personal touch will be lost.

Once you've started an affair with your boss, do your best to keep it out of working hours, no matter how much both of you may feel like a passionate bout of petting in the storeroom. It will keep him interested—having you around but officially untouchable—and it will also prevent the affair from becoming a company scandal, which could give him a good reason for dropping you like a hot potato.

Don't sit on his lap for dictation. Don't grope him when you're handing him his letters. Give him a little kiss when nobody's likely to be looking, but leave it at that. Another point: if he's married and his wife telephones, resist the temptation to roll your eyes up and say, "It's *her*," no matter how much he may have run her down to you. If you've taken him on, you've taken him on in his married situation, and you'll have to accept that his relationship with his wife still exists. No matter what he's said, he won't respect you for criticizing his spouse—your attitude may even send him back into her arms.

Supposing that every man you work with is ancient, ugly, or married to the point of insensibility? Then you'll have to go on the prowl elsewhere, and that, although it's often quicker, can have just as many pitfalls.

As I said before, men often lack self-confidence, and although they may approach you, and chat with you, they need definite and unmistakable signs that you're interested—if you are. One of the best seduction techniques is the glance across the crowded room. If you see a man looking at you with obvious interest, and you're attracted to him as well, develop the tactic of staring at him just a little longer and little more frequently than you normally would.

After a while, allow yourself the ghost of a smile.

Glances like these, and small encouraging grins, have an electrifying effect on most men. They're really flattered by it. The reason for this is, traditionally it's been men who eye women, and not the other way around. At any rate, that's how a lot of men perceive things. They don't think of themselves as being attractive in the same way that a woman thinks of herself. If a woman walks into a crowded room with her hair beautifully coiffed and a plunging-neckline dress on, she expects people to turn around and stare at her. No matter how good-looking a man is, he doesn't expect to be ogled in the same way.

Another advantage of the lingering look is that it shows you're interested without you having to commit yourself too much, or risk looking promiscuous and undignified. All it does is open the way for the man to approach you and start talking.

Don't underestimate how much a man can be put off by an apparent display of coolness. That doesn't mean you have to slaver over him as though your pants are permanently on fire. Just drop him a little encouragement now and again, or he may lose his nerve and decide that, much as he's attracted to you, he can't stand the tension and the embarrassment. Just because he's not smooth and glib at first doesn't necessarily mean that he has nothing to say for himself. Give him a chance, and you'll be surprised how much he responds to it and appreciates it.

What should you do if you walk into a dance or party and see a man surrounded by beautiful woman, and find that you crave him to the point of distraction? How can you make an extra-special impression on him?

If he's the kind of guy who is used to having a swarm of fawning females around, it's the Koh-I-Noor to a piece of Bazooka bubble gum that there's one thing he *isn't* used to. Something that, if handled properly, he could find extremely provocative and attractive.

That something is *argument*.

When you argue with somebody, the adrenalin starts flowing in both of your bodies, and the nervous system quickens your pulse, rate of breathing, and other basic functions. Among other things, these physical responses have the effect of titillating the pleasure areas in the brain, and so when you start arguing with a man, you will often be giving him an actual pleasurable kick—a kick he never gets out of women who dote on him and agree with everything he says.

So join the circle of admirers, listen to what's going on, and then start butting in. But don't get *too* excited, too shrill, or too femininely hysterical. Keep your cool, and be persistently contradictory. In the end, you'll find that he's giving all his attention to you, because he wants to put his point of view over to you, and he also finds the argument exciting. You become a challenge to his masculinity, and he will make an extra effort with you. The stage is set for attraction, reaction ... and seduction.

Men are flattered by women who come running at their beck and call, but they're fascinated by women who won't.

How open you are in your sexual approaches to men is up to you. But be prepared to reap what you have sown. If you flicker your eyelashes at a man, and waggle your rump, and press your breasts against his arm, don't go all horrified and coy if he wants to fuck you. He's only responding to what have been quite obvious mating signals. You can *flirt* with men: they enjoy it, and I know that sure as hell you enjoy it. Everybody likes to be admired and cause a stir. But don't systematically lead a man on to the point where he thinks he has an easy lay all lined up. Women like that end up in the middle of unpleasant scenes, or with black eyes and broken noses, or (worse still) dead. A classic pattern of murders involving rape is that a man has been led to expect that he might get more from a girl than she's really prepared to give.

If you're fortunate enough to be surrounded by a crowd of men, resist, please resist, the temptation to laugh louder and show off and generally play up to it. Not to put too fine a point on it, men who see you doing that will think you're an idiot.

The woman who attracts men the most is the woman who looks encouraging and promising but definitely has something in reserve, something that arouses the male response to a challenge. She's sexy without being nymphomaniac, outspoken without being shrill, and she knows just the right times to open those melting eyes of her and listen as he fires off some boastful little story about how he tuned up his Mustang Mach 2 and beat out everybody else on the turnpike. Men love talking about themselves and their achievements, and they love a woman who listens to them. Beware, though, of the less confident guy who talks about what he's done in a *negative* way. "I wrote a play but I don't suppose they'll accept it," he says. *Don't* say, "Oh, what a pity." Instead, say, "That's the trouble with television these days—they don't appreciate good writing when they see it." You get the message?

There are ways of being positively physical with a man that will turn him on just as much as waving a pair of 38D's under his nose. If you're attracted to him, even though you've only just met him, you can do things like stroking the side of his hair, saying, "Do you know you're going just a little bit gray? I think that's really nice." Apart from the compliment, which is fairly meaningless, he will have felt your fingers through his hair, and that can be a very erotic sensation. When he lights your cigarette, hold his wrist. When you cross the room with him, or introduce him to someone you know, take his hand.

I've often recommended a pretense of a knowledge of palmistry as a good opening technique for seduction. The palm of the hand is very sensitive, and as you trace his lifelines and lovelines or whatever, you can stroke his hand with your fingers. People are like animals—they get inordinate pleasure out of being fondled. Under the guise of doing something quite remote and intellectual, you can be stimulating a man in the most basic and animal way possible.

Dancing with a man is an excellent way to bring out his lustful instincts, as you've probably realized. I've often found it amusing to look at a dance floor crowded with clinging couples and try to guess how many men have erections. Dancing gives you the excuse to use, in a dignified way, the very down-home technique that clip-joint hostesses use on their gullible male customers. Under cover of the tablecloth, they open his pants and start to masturbate him, but at the first indication that he's not going to buy them one more bottle of champagne, they stop. Subtle use of your thighs while you're dancing can have almost exactly the same effect.

What about picking up men in the street, or at airports or bus terminals? You don't have to be a hooker to feel attracted to a man you see in a crowd and to want to talk to him. At airports, one of the favorite methods is to approach a man, wearing a very anxious look, and ask him whether he'd mind helping you to choose some after-shave lotion for your brother. You don't really know what fragrances men like, and you do need help. Apart from the flattery of being asked for his advice, the man will inevitably respond to the intimate business of sniffing wrists.

If you see a man in the street and you find him attractive, simply approach him and ask him where he bought his hat/jacket/raincoat, because your brother (listen, you don't actually have to *have* a brother) has been wanting one for a long time, and his birthday is coming up soon. Don't just ask directions, or the time, or something brief and simple like that—ask something that needs a lengthy explanation, so that he'll have the chance to hold forth for a while and realize what a good listener you are, and how much of an impression he's making on you.

The important factor in all these pickup techniques I've described is that they don't rob you of your mystery or dignity, or leave anyone thinking you're a pushy whore. All they do is open the way for the man to be able to make a move. The actual invitation will be his, and he'll never even realize just how much he's been set up to make it.

Many women seem to have firmly lodged in their heads the curious idea that if they invite a man back to their apartment, they have to cook an amazing four-course meal, serve it graciously by candlelight, and prove their prowess as a hostess and gourmet chef.

Sometimes I sit back and think of all those dimly lit rooms all over the city where couples are spooning up vichyssoise and wishing they were in bed instead.

Once you've located and attracted the man you want, and feel like having him home for bed, then for God's sake have him home for bed and don't worry about having to prove that you're the greatest cook since Escoffier. A primly set table, with napkins and knives and forks and sideplates and everything else, becomes a hurdle in your lovemaking. The man won't want to throw you into bed immediately because he doesn't want to hurt your feelings by letting your elaborate dinner go cold, and also he might have the suspicion (unfounded or not) that you're trying to show him what an excellent wife you'd make. For some men (not all) this could cause a definite cooling of ardor.

Make sure your apartment is tidy, warm, and feminine. Have a couple of bottles of wine or liquor around. Bring in a couple of pizzas, or some bread and cheese, or maybe a couple of quick-braising steaks with a salad, but don't go overboard on the food. It's you he wants, not your comestibles.

This is the time when you can really dress sexily. A long backless satin dress, perhaps, worn without a bra. A frilled low-cut blouse and ankle-length skirt. Tight slacks and a glittery tank top.

Concentrate on having beautiful hair and perfect eye makeup. Underneath, wear slinky and expensive panties, but don't try and be tarty-sexy and wear a G-string or anything like that. Kinky undies are terrific for erotic love games, which could come later in your relationship, but at the moment you're trying to play the part of the smooth, desirable girl who is available for seduction—not the know-it-all hooker who's ready for anything.

When your target for tonight arrives at your apartment, do everything you can to make him relax. Don't disappear into the kitchen and tell him to fix his own drink. Stay with him, take his jacket, and pour him what he wants. Show that you're interested enough to want to know what he's been doing since you last saw him. Ask him if he's hungry, but if he's not, don't worry about it. You're not his mother.

Once he's relaxed, you can relax, and that's when the lovemaking can begin . . .

# 7.

## *How to Choose Your Lover*

Accidents, happy or otherwise, usually decide who you're going to have sex with in this life and who you're not. A woman I knew used to sit by her window and say, with a deep and soulful sigh, "Just think. There are millions of good-looking men out there, and I'll never get to bed with more than a handful."

Since this is (sadly) true, you can see how important it is that you choose your own handful well. A sterile and ineffectual sex relationship is a waste of time, a waste of youth, and a waste of your potential as a sexually oriented woman.

You won't always be lucky enough to find the kind of man who will buy you diamonds and dinners, owns oil wells for a hobby, and makes the earth move each and every time you make love. But if you're sensible (which you won't always be), you can at least cut down the possibility of losing hours of precious time on sexual flops and emotional deadbeats.

The external appearances of men, as you've probably found out, can be extremely deceptive. Behind the wheel of a Cadillac Coupe de Ville, wearing stern dark sunglasses and clanking with masterful ID bracelets and neck chains, may often sit a small and neurotic little boy, whose sexual performance is still paddling around in adolescent incompetence. Whereas the quiet unassuming librarian in rimless glasses and with too-short hair might well have the biggest dong this side of the Washington Monument, and know how to use it, too.

This is only supposition, of course. It could be the other way around.

But what *isn't* supposition is that certain types of men are, sexually, better bets than others, and since social decorum usually denies you the chance of measuring a man's cock before you decide to get to know him intimately, it's useful to know in advance what type of man he's likely to be.

I can't predict what strange chances will befall you in your love life. Neither do I know what your personal preferences are in men, and whether the kind of man *I* would consider to be totally unsuitable and unlikely would be the kind of man who would sweep *you* off your feet.

But, being a man myself, and therefore possessing a little inside information on the sexual motivation of men, I can at least give you due warning of certain types of men that you would be well advised to approach with caution. And which types of men, of course, can be almost guaranteed to give you a good time.

I've prepared this chapter as a kind of free-form questionnaire, since a man's sexual personality is something you just can't be dogmatic and black-and-white about. The purpose of the questionnaire is only to tell you whether the man is likely to be a good lover, sexually and emotionally, and it is not intended to cast any aspersions on his other talents and abilities. He might be terrible in bed, but he might be excellent at card games, and what's the good of a tremendous lover if all you want is a bridge partner?

As you go through the questions, keep track of the score you think the man you have in mind deserves, and at the finish of the chapter you'll be able to add up his score and see how he rates. A word of advice: Make your score marks in soft pencil, and erase them immediately afterward. This is the kind of book that men pick up to see what designs you have on them, and if he sees how you've scored him, he may take offense. It's always easier to be honest about someone else than it is about yourself.

First of all, let's take a look at *clothing*. Would you say your intended lover is dress-conscious (3), too dressy (2), or too sloppy (1)? Do his pants touch his shoes (2) or not (1)? Does he wear clashing plaids, checks, and stripes (1) or not (2)? Are his lapels narrow (1) or wide (2)? Does he wear short-sleeved shirts (1) or not (2)? Does he wear violent ties (1) or not (2)? Does he wear an undershirt (1) or not (2)? Are his pants tapered (1) or flared (2)? Are his shoes pointed (1) or rounded (2)? Do his socks match his pants (3) his shoes (2) or neither (1)? If he wears glasses, are they nondescript (1) or stylish (2)? Does he wear jewelry—rings (2), ID bracelet (1) or neck chain (0)? Are his pants baggy in the seat (1) or not (2)? Does the outline of his cock show through his pants clearly (1) faintly (2) or not at all (0)?

Apart from these salient points about his clothes, which have been assembled with the help of two fashion journalists and a tailor, and which throw a spotlight on the weakest points of most men's dress, there are general things to watch for when you're assessing a potential lover. Are his clothes expensive and new (3)? Cheap and new (2)? Old but expensive (2)? Cheap and old (1)?

Do you think that he dresses the right way for his age and lifestyle? Does he dress too young for his age (1)? Too formal (1)? Too casual—jeans and sweatshirt (1)? Too old (1)? Or do you think he dresses just right (2)?

Clothes are a vital clue to a man's sexual personality because they are his public face. They represent, in terms of cloth, cut, and color, the kind of impression that the man wants to give about his personality to the outside world. If he is fashion-conscious, careful about matching his clothes, and his clothes looked reasonably well cared for and costly, then he is more likely to be a better lover. He cares about the impression he is making on other people, and he also likes to feel good and relaxed. What's more, if he doesn't mind spending good money on clothes, then he certainly won't mind spending some on you. If you're interested in a well-heeled lover, though, make sure that his clothes really *are* new, and aren't meticulously cared-for older clothes. You can make a spot check on this by looking at the inside lining of his jacket. If it's creased at the edges, the jacket has been dry-cleaned quite a few times. As you run your hands sensuously down his jacket front, you can also subtly raise his lapel and see if the fabric color *under* the lapel matches the surrounding fabric. Fabric fades in sun and weather. Worn shoes are another big give-away.

A woman I knew (admittedly an out-and-out gold-digger) always used to ask her men friends to take off their jackets and relax when they came around for drinks. Any man whose jacket sported less than an Yves St. Laurent or Saville Row label suddenly used to find that the martinis weren't the only icy feature of her apartment.

Men who are too dressy are usually lacking in self-confidence in their sexual personality and are trying to make up for it by putting on extra-sharp duds. They can also be vain and introverted, often more interested in you as a decorative appendage to their ensemble rather than a real, live woman. Never try to seduce a man who, at any other time apart from weddings and other family celebrations, wears a flower in his buttonhole.

Men who are too sloppy are usually too sloppy in one of two different ways. Either they are trying to acquire a rugged look (studded denim jacket, big leather buckle, boots and jeans) or else they simply have no interest in how they look (unpressed slacks, crumpled jackets, shapeless shirts, hopelessly chaotic mixtures of plaids and checks and spots and stripes). Those men who are *trying* to look rugged can often be quite good lovers, but rarely for very long. They have a virility hangup which is often rooted in an inability to get on well with women, and that's why they try to appear all craggy and remote. It's the only way they can handle women—by being aggressive. The men who are sloppy because they simply don't care occasionally make wonderful lifetime partners. They're the raw material of steady, dependable husbands. They usually make appallingly bad lovers, simply because they're not aware of the impression they're making on you—visually, emotionally, or physically.

Okay, that's a quick rundown on clothes. There's also *personal hygiene* to be considered. I know some women like funky, male-smelling lovers, but do try and think about the morning after, when you wake up next to a rancid armpit, being breathed over in steady blasts by a mouth that last tasted Crest on Thanksgiving Day, 1973. David Loovis, author of the homosexual version of *The Sensuous Woman, Gay Spirit,* thinks armpits are wonderful—"Think of his armpits as hanging gardens." All I can say to *that* is that it depends on what kind of a hanging garden you're faced with—a rose bower or a compost heap.

Are his fingernails clean and short (2) or dirty and uneven (1)? Are his toenails kempt (2) or not (1)? Is he shaved (or beard trimmed) (2), or unshaven and untidy (1)? Is his hair clean (2) or greasy (1)? Does he use a deodorant (2) or not (1)? After-shave (2) or not (1)? Is he generally tidy (2) or untidy (1)?

The simple principle behind those questions is that if a man can't be bothered to be nice to know, then he's usually *not* nice to know. You may at first be turned on by his Neanderthal hygiene, but I warn you here and now that after a couple of weeks you'll be offering him bribes just to take *one* eentsy-weentsy shower.

On the other hand, of course, beware the man who smells overpoweringly of perfume. Either he's semi-gay, or he's vain and self-centered, or he's worried about a personal odor which you haven't noticed yet, or else he has no sense of smell. It might be *all* of these, in which case you'd be better off dating your Neanderthal.

While you're checking over his personal hygiene, you can also look out for little *personal habits*. What does he do with his hands when he's talking? Does he cover his mouth with his hand (1) or not (2)? Does he scratch his head (2) or not (1)? Does he keep emphasizing everything he says by pointing at you (1) or not (2)?

Does he spread his hands apart appealingly when he makes a conversational point (2) or not (1)? Does he pound his clenched fist on the table (1) or not (2)? Does he dig in his ears (1) or not (2)? Does he move his hands rhythmically with his speech (2) or not (1)? Does he sit with his arms folded (1) or not (2)? Does he look directly at you when he talks (2) or not (1)? Does he look up and down your body as he talks (1) or not (2)? Is he relaxed when he talks to you (2) or not (1)? Does he lean forward when you lean forward, and lean back when you lean back, as you talk to each other (2) or not (1)? Does he move around so that he puts himself between you and other people (2) or not (1)? Any little seductive habits—like licking his lips, flashing his eyes, or little smiles (2) or not (1)?

These actions mostly come under the heading of body language. They are unconscious actions which a man may or may not perform when he meets you, and they show whether or not he's interested in you sexually, and how much. It's impossible to delve into the pyschology of all these gestures, but two of the most interesting are the folded-arms gesture, which represents a deliberate shutout of you and your sex appeal, and the lean-forward lean-back gesture. Recent American communications research has shown that people perform complicated "dances" when they speak to each other, and that if they are locked into each other's wavelength, they will mirror each other's gestures. They will lean forward toward each other at precisely the same split-second (as action-replay movies have demonstrated). If a man is *not* interested, he will remain still, or involved in a "dance" of his own.

Men who keep pointing their finger at you are generally the same with their cocks. They are aggressive thrusters who might be all right for a one-night stand, but whose constant emphatic monotone begins to pall after the tenth emphatic bout. Men who cover their mouths with their hands when they talk are lacking in self-confidence, or else their dentures are about to drop out.

The topics of *conversation* that a man launches into

when he meets you are also important clues to his sexual personality and approach. Few men are really adept at the kind of flowing, piquant conversation that sweeps you away and makes you feel flattered and provoked at the same time, but nonetheless you should be able to judge something of his erotic powers by the pearls that droppeth from his lips.

Does he talk more about you (3) or more about himself (1) or more about something else altogether (2)? Does he talk about his work (1) or not (2)? Does he gossip about people *you* don't know, but *he* does (1) or not (2)? Does he make you laugh (2) or not (1)? Do you think his conversation is sexually suggestive (1) or not (2)? Does he compliment you (2) or not (1)? Does he seem to have a bee in his bonnet about one particular subject (1) or not (2)? Do you feel he has bottled up a tide of conversation that he's been dying to tell someone (1) or not (2)? Does he talk to you as though he's a teacher and you're the pupil (2) or not (1)? Does he seem to have rigid views (1) or not (2)? Does he talk about sex easily (2) or does it make him uncomfortable (1)? Does he clam up when someone else joins in the conversation (1) or not (2)? Does he do very much more talking than you (1), about the same (3) or very much less. (2)?

The point of assessing his conversation is to see whether he's the kind of man who has a one-track mind (doggedly devoted to his career, or to his sport, or to his car), in which case you have little hope of becoming anything more than a second-class interest in his life. If he burbles on about duck shooting when he's meeting you for the first time, what the hell is he going to be like after three months?

You will also be able to judge the nature and broadness of his education. You will want to know the *nature* of his education because it will give you solid information about his upbringing. Advanced classics scholars may not all be clumsy lovers, but you have to devote a great deal of mental energy to Ancient Greek, and that means he has probably spent more time honing his vocabulary than honing his penis. I'm not dogmatically suggesting that an unhoned penis is necessarily a bad thing, but if it's *skill* you're looking for, you have to accept that *experience* is a prerequisite.

*Avoid,* on the whole, mathematicians, physics majors, chemistry buffs, engineers, insurance assessors, classicists, policemen, tree surgeons, beekeepers, mechanics of all varieties, sports reporters, plastic surgeons, veterinarians, and realtors. They have very little in common except that their mental attitudes and their professions *tend* to make them obsessive, incompetent, disinterested, or hyperpragmatic in bed. Before I am inundated with furious letters from the wives of beekeepers, telling me how sensual and arousing their spouses are, I must emphasize that these are only tendencies, for use as a quick "shall-I, shan't-I" seduction guide. And anyway, if you know anything about beekeeping, you'll know that the world's greatest beekeeper is a German—and a monk.

Try and ask your lover-to-be a few sharp questions about sex. The way that a man talks about sex is a big giveaway to his erotic attitudes. If he's calm and relaxed about it but smiles a lot, then he's at home with the subject and he also likes you steering the conversation that way. In other words, he's interested in you, and could be a good lover. If he talks *too* dirty, then he's probably more than a little frustrated, and he's probably one of those boring men who get a kick out of trying to shock women with naughty language. Tell him to go and get you another martini, then melt into the crowd when he's gone. If he blushes and stammers, you'd better forget it for tonight.

About those sharp questions: ask him, for instance, what he'd say to a woman just after making love. Ask him, too, what he'd do if he were caught in bed with a woman by her husband/lover. I'm afraid to say that when it happened to me I hid in a large closet. Yes, really.

Test a man's interest in the *sensual pleasures* of life. Does he like good food (2) or not (1)? Does he enjoy good wine (2) or not (1)? Does he like art (2) or not

(1)? Men who snatch hot dogs for lunch and wash them down with Miller's High Life are not known for their sensuality.

Check out his *car*. Women don't often understand this technique, because they don't see the same things in cars as men do. As sales research has shown, women buy cars (on the whole) for their cosmetic appearance *or* for their economy in size and fuel. The twin influences, I guess, of years of putting on makeup and balancing the household books.

Men, on the other hand, buy cars because they directly reflect, in metal and glass, what facade they want to present to the world. Part of the sales motivation is therefore cosmetic, which means that an aggressive radiator grille and lots of headlights are important to men, but part of it is concerned with *the power of the engine*, which is something that not many women are into. If you want to check your potential lover's sexual aggression rating, you will have to find out the horsepower of his car engine. A man who believes he's adequate in bed will not be content with a car that won't haul him up an incline. But there comes a point beyond which a car has more power than is either adequate or sensible, and men who drive cars like that tend to be sexually impotent lovers who are trying to compensate for their inadequacy with extra horsepower.

This theory of mine has yet to be proved scientifically. But I have tested it myself with over a hundred drivers that I know personally, and I always check on the physical appearance of drivers in high-powered cars. Almost without exception, they are aging or unfit, and unfitness generally means inadequate sexual performance. Remember again that this is a rule-of-thumb guide to help you make a quick decision, and that there are bound to be notable exceptions to the rule.

Award your lover-to-be, then, the following marks. If he drives an average American sedan, give him (2) for 250 hp, (3) for 330 hp, and (1) for 380 hp (all at 5,000 rpm). If he drives any British or Japanese sports car, award him (2). If he drives a Ferrari, a Lamborghini, or a Ford GT40, give him (1).

*Books* and *records* will tell you more and more about your potential lover. They will give you some idea, of course, whether he shares any of the same tastes as you. But they will also give away his sexual likes and dislikes, and hint at his bedtime prowess.

Are his books mainly paperbacks (1) mainly hardbacks (2) or a mix of both (3)? Are they mainly fiction (1) mainly nonfiction (2) or a mix of both (3)? Does he read more thrillers and sci-fi books than anything else (1) or not (2)? Does he read all the fashionable bestsellers, such as *Gravity's Rainbow* and *Watership Down* (1) or does he read unusual titles that are not on the best-seller lists (2)? Does he own any art or antiques books (2) or not (1)? Any sex books (2) or not (1)? Are his records mainly classical (1) mainly pop (1) or a mix of both (2)? Are his pop records reasonably up to date (2) or not (1)? Are his classical records familiar (1) or not (2)?

This test has nothing to do with intellectual snobbery, but simply to tell whether your lover-to-be has an inquiring mind, and whether he has his own tastes, or if he reads and listens to whatever the critics tell him to read or listen to. Men with inquiring minds tend to be more creative about sex and usually make better lovers. The types of books and records he's into are also important. If he gets a kick out of finicky philosophical discussion, or revels in the ordered construction of Bach organ recitals, then he may be a little fussier and a little less physically oriented than a jazz or rock lover, or a man who reads J. P. Donleavy.

If you had the time, you could strip a man and his possessions right down to the bone and discover almost exactly what kind of a lover he would probably be. But, like most major decisions in life, choosing your bed partners usually has to be a snap judgment, and that's why I've assembled this quick and easy questionnaire. It is necessarily unfair to Volkswagen-driving Latin scholars with odd socks and a taste for Mickey Spillane, but you could argue that they're being pretty unfair to themselves, let alone the community at large.

The maximum score possible for the questions I've asked in this chapter is 133. If your lover-to-be racks up the whole 133, then you have my permission to go to bed with him even before you've finished reading this book, because he's undoubtedly worth laying your hands on at once. He's wide-awake, sensual, sensitive without being neurotic, and is probably a terrific fuck.

Any score over 100 is good, and if you're inclined to favor the man, then I recommend acceptance of his overtures. Anything between 80 and 100 is not bad, and if you're frustrated and stuck for an amusing short-term lover, this might be your man. Between 50 and 80 you are pushing your luck. Under 50, and it would be wiser to leave this man for the attentions of a motherly spinster from Twin Forks.

No quiz can tell you conclusively whether the men you meet are right for you or not. But the information you will be noting and sifting through with this questionnaire will at least be marginally more analytical than the kind of random data that people usually pick up about each other when they first meet. One woman, now divorced, told me what she recalled when she first met her ex-husband: "It was his eyes—they were such a beautiful green, and they looked so sincere. I think if he'd had brown eyes I wouldn't have fallen for him."

If only she'd just sneaked a look under his lapels, or at the heels of his shoes. If she'd only assessed the horsepower of his car and checked his taste in music.

No decision of such personal importance as making up your mind whether a man is going to be your lover or not is undertaken with such cursory thought and care. He's going to share your bed. His penis is going to slide inside your vagina. He might stay with you for six months. He might stay with you for the rest of your life. And you don't even know whether his family has hereditary schizophrenia or not, let alone whether he files his nails regularly.

Maybe this questionnaire won't convince you the first

time. Maybe it won't convince you the second time. But maybe the *third* time, when you're making the rating of yet another possible bedmate, you'll begin to think that although life is full of happy accidents, it's sometimes worth looking where you're going.

# 8.

## *Time for Love*

"When am'rous John in glowing hopes draws near;
    If my fair front to his I shall incline
He'll say I'm bold and turn his head aside,
And think he's purchased a lascivious bride.
But that I no apology may lack
I'm e'en resolved to lie upon my back."

—Anonymous, 19th century

That rhyme, which appeared in a bawdy London magazine of the last century, rather neatly sums up the problem that faces a woman when it's time for her to have sex with her lover.

While men usually do not like a woman who lies still and submissive and who doesn't actively join in, they still have deep-seated prejudices against women who know too much. It is important to the male sexual ego—and because of that, to the male erection—that a man feels he is dominant in bed, and that he is *teaching* the woman things that she doesn't already know.

Although it seems hopelessly chauvinistic and out-dated, I cannot emphasize enough how important it is that a man still has some feeling that he is introducing his woman to sexual delights that she has never tried before. These days, men are reconciled to the fact that they're probably not the first, but they still want to be the best.

The roots of this feeling go back as far as recorded history. Read any erotic literature of any period, and it's obvious that what thrills men most of all is the idea of despoiling a virgin, of thrusting their enormous pricks into tight and untried territory. Here's a typical extract, from a long Victorian novel called *Rose d'Amour:*

> No sooner did I feel the head lodged aright that I drove and shoved in with the utmost fury; feeling the head pretty well in I trust and drove on, but gained so little that I drew it out, and wetting it with spittle I again effect the lodgement just within the lips. At length by my fierce rending and tearing thrusts the first defenses gave way. I now recommenced my eager shoves, my fierce lungings, and I felt my self gaining at every move, till with one tremendous and cunt-rending thrust I buried myself in her up to the hilt. So great was the pain of this last shock that Rose could not suppress a sharp shrill scream, but I heeded it not: it was the note of final victory.

Now I don't expect you to try and pretend that you're a virgin when you go to bed with the man you want (unless, of course, you are). But you can strike a happy medium between lustfulness and coyness. If you're too rampant and aggressive, you may make him feel sexually inexperienced and inferior, and feelings like that have a definite depressive effect on the male erection.

When you've maneuvered a date with the man you want, you'll probably find that you can let him set the pace of petting. When you're kissing, he'll want to caress you and fondle your breasts, and he'll inevitably try to put his hand up your skirt or dress. Resist him—just enough to make him feel that he's having to work for his oats. When he finally manages to slip his fingers into your panties, he'll feel pleased with himself, and a feeling of self-satisfaction and conquest does wonders for his virility.

At the petting stage, you'll build up much more erotic tension if you try and keep your hands off his penis. Unbutton his shirt and caress his chest—run your fingers down to his stomach and around his naked back—but apart from a few "accidental" brushes against the rising bulge in his pants, leave his cock alone. He'll want you to touch it and handle it all the more, and the erotic suspense will make him even more passionate.

When you're both ready for bed, and the lights are low, and Mantovani is pouring musical treacle from the record player, let him undress you. Remember that he may need a little subtle help, because men's fingers are bigger and clumsier than yours, and you may have small buttons and hooks-and-eyes that give him problems. If he's at all experienced, he will know how to divest you of your duds, but there are many fashionable clothes that men find confusing. Lead his fingers gently to your side zippers if he can't locate them; pull your elasticated cuffs over your hands so that he doesn't try and tug your sleeves off inside out.

While he's doing this, keep on kissing and caressing him, and start to take off his clothes as well. Unbutton his shirt, undo his cuffs (watch for cufflinks, some have a swing bar on the back and others push through like buttons), and slide his shirt off his back while you're kissing him. If he knows what he's doing, he should have taken his shoes and socks off by himself, and it's not worth trying to take off his pants until he has. Even though he may wear bell-bottoms, you'll both get into a hopeless tangle, and he'll be falling around like an idiot with his trousers halfway down his legs. Keeping your dignity is a very important part of undressing.

When you're ready to undo his pants, fondle his erect penis through the fabric before you start, to add that extra modicum of excitement. Then unclip or unbuckle his trouser fastening, open his zipper, and slide one hand in under his balls, outside his underpants. With the other hand, take his trousers down past his hips, he'll kick them off himself past his knees and ankles.

Stroke and squeeze his penis even more through his underpants, and then slip your hands inside and take them down. If this is a first date, resist any temptation you might feel to kneel down and take his cock in your mouth. That can come later, when he guides you into doing it. To begin with, it's a little too bold and a little too abrupt. He doesn't want to think he's dated a push-over.

By now, you should both be naked and ready for the delights of foreplay.

Actually, I don't know who the hell called it *foreplay*, because to most people that suggests something you do early, a kind of warming up before the real event. As far as I'm concerned, erotic play should continue throughout the act of love, and for that reason I always call it *loveplay*. So many books about sex divide the procedure up as though you're actually supposed to stop tickling and caressing and kissing when Intercourse Proper begins, even though it's really an essential adjunct to what you're doing.

During the early stages of loveplay, you can arouse a man's passion and excitement without actually handling his penis. Kiss him, deeply and erotically, and thrust your tongue in his mouth. Lick his face—even his eyes if you want to—an unusual caress that some men find extremely sexy. Run your fingernails caressingly over his back and sides, and nip his neck and shoulders with your teeth. Suck and bite his nipples.

By shifting your thighs, or pressing your stomach against his, you can give his penis subtle caresses and stimulation, enough to ensure that his erection remains powerful and hard.

Work your hands down his back, pinching and scratching him gently, and around his bottom. Run one pointed nail down the crack of his behind, just momentarily goosing his anus, and then fondle his balls from the back. Reach the other hand around to the front, and take hold of his cock.

Now there's a whole lot written about how to hold a man's penis, and many women are rather scared to try, in case they do it wrong. Because of this, most inexperienced girls don't hold a man's penis hard enough, and their caresses are more frustrating than arousing.

As we've seen, the most sensitive part of the penis is the head, or glans. The actual shaft of it is not nearly so sensitive, and can be gripped quite tightly. All men have masturbated at one time or another, and they're used to their own firm handhold, so yours will hardly be able to hurt him.

The best way to hold your lover's penis, if you're lying next to him, is to rest your thumb against the bulge of the glans, and curl the rest of your fingers around the underside of the shaft, with the pad of your index finger lightly touching that sensitive little string of skin that runs from the opening in his penis to the shaft itself. Rub him up and down firmly and evenly and as quickly as you like (although don't go mad if you think he's close to climax—you don't want him to shoot his wad before he's even entered you).

If he's lying on his back on the bed, and you're kneeling beside him, you can hold his penis the other way around—that is, with your thumb on his frenum and the rest of your fingers around the top of the shaft. Don't worry about changing hands if one of them gets tired, that's quite okay. A really experienced lover can rub her man's penis at a rate of 250 strokes a minute, and believe me, that feels like something.

You don't necessarily have to use your fingers to stimulate his penis, either. You can roll it against your thigh with the palm of your hand; you can press it and squeeze it and rub it between your breasts. A technique that most men find extremely arousing is to have their penis caressed through your hair—you can wrap it around his cock and massage him with your hand, while kissing his balls at the same time.

You can hold his cock between your legs without actually insterting it into your vagina, and using a circular motion of your thighs, rub it against your clitoris and pubic hair. S'nice.

Don't ignore his anus, either. The anus is packed with nerves that can give a man very erotic feelings. You can stroke it and pinch it, and a trick that's extremely arousing is to dip your middle finger in the juice from your own vagina and thrust it up his ass. Contrary to widely held belief, the rectum is not full of feces until you're actually having a bowel movement. If your lover is reasonably clean, the anus is generally quite empty, so you won't emerge with a shit-smeared finger. Sorry to be so basic, but it's something worth knowing.

Cunnilingus (your lover licking your vulva and clitoris with his tongue) and fellatio (you stimulating your lover's penis with your mouth) are both important and integral parts of loveplay. Fellatio is something every woman who wants to drive her man wild in bed should be good at, and although it takes some courage to do it for the first time, most women find it extremely arousing and enjoyable once they've gotten used to it.

You may find that your first opportunity to fellate your lover comes when he starts licking you. Incidentally, don't be embarrassed and coy if he tries to do this, and don't push him away. While you may never have had a man licking you between the legs before, it shows how much he feels for you, and that he finds the whole of your body attractive and arousing.

If he's giving you cunnilingus in what's called the "69" position—that is, with his feet next to your head, so that together you form a shape rather like the numbers 69—you'll find that his erect penis is bobbing around in close proximity to your mouth. Take it in your hand, and try licking the end of it and giving it little kisses. Then open your mouth and draw your lips in around your teeth, so that you won't bite him, and take the head of his cock in.

Although it's colloquially called "cocksucking," fellatio is not actual sucking. Some girls suck and suck on their unfortunate lover's penis until he feels he's having an affair with a vacuum cleaner. It hardly stimulates his cock at all, and it can even be painful.

You can give his penis a few gentle sucks, and you'll probably need to when your mouth fills with saliva and the few drops of lubricant juice that emerge from the end of his cock. But most of the time, you should be drawing the glans in and out of your mouth, caressing it with your lips, and using your tongue to probe the tiny opening, the frenum, and the corona.

Many men enjoy having their penis "strummed" by a fast-flickering tongue as you fellate them, and as you grow more and more experienced, you'll find ways of rolling your tongue around his cock while you're giving him head until he doesn't know whether he's coming or going. You can also slide your mouth down the shaft, and lick and suck his balls.

A word of warning: *be careful* when you take his balls into your mouth. They are extremely sensitive, and while this can give him a sensation like the bottom's dropped out of his scrotum, it can also give him an unpleasant pain, followed by persistent ballsache. Unless you have a mouth that's used to swallowing jelly donuts whole, don't attempt to take in both balls at once.

While you're around the area of the balls, you can lick and gently bite with your teeth the little region between balls and anus, the perineum. Then you can go on, if you like, to give him what they call "a trip around the world," or anilingus. Lick and nip his anus, and forming your tongue into a rigid U-shape, see how far you can push it up his bottom. It'll give him a warm wet slithery feeling in his backside that will endear him to you for a long time.

Meanwhile, back at your frantic fellatio, your sophisticated oral caresses have aroused him to the point of climax. You'll know when he's ready, because the juices from his cock will start to flow a little, and the cock itself will grow harder and tenser and seem to fill your mouth right up.

Question: if he climaxes, should you take his sperm in your mouth, and if you do, should you swallow it?

Sperm is white, jellyish, stringy, and has a faintly bleachy smell and a rather astringent effect on the mouth. Apart from submicroscopic spermatozoa, those tiny tadpoles that fertilize your eggs, it contains nothing more exciting than protein and simple sugars. Despite persistent rumors, it does not enlarge the bust, nor can you become pregnant from swallowing it. The nearest sensation to swallowing sperm is taking down a teaspoonful of raw egg white. (Incidentally, don't swallow it if you're more than seven months' pregnant—it contains substances that could bring on premature labor).

It's my belief that no man should force a girl to swallow his semen. It is very exciting and flattering when a girl does it, and it somehow makes the act of fellatio seem more complete, but don't feel that you have to against your will. Some men will be tricky enough to hold your head just when they're coming, so be on your guard for that. A quick turn to the side will safeguard your virgin throat.

But I do think that any girl who wants to consider herself a sophisticated lover should develop the art of swallowing sperm. It's no good holding your nose and taking it down like medicine, however. If you're going to swallow it, learn to enjoy it.

Tricia, 22, learned to drink semen and influence people like this:

"First of all, I'd take Simon's cock out of my mouth just before he was about to come, and let it all spurt over my face and lips. He didn't mind that, because it looked really sexy, and it gave me the chance to stick the tip of my tongue out and have just a little *taste*.

"Then I started swallowing a little bit, and letting the rest of it run out of the side of my mouth. It turned him on to see me doing that, too, so he didn't feel I was being fastidious or rejecting him or anything. In the end, I got so used to it that I found I could take all of it down, and didn't mind it in the least. In fact I've grown quite used to the taste of it now. It's like learning to eat shellfish and oysters: you don't know how on earth you're going to manage at first, and then you end up really looking forward to them."

Here's another little trick, which your lover, if he's reasonably sophisticated, will appreciate: with his sperm still in your mouth, move up and give him a deep kiss. It has to be one of the most intimate gestures of all time. Similarly, if he's been licking you, and his mouth is glistening with your love-juice, don't hesitate to kiss him then. You may not like the taste of yourself as much as he does, but it will give him a kick.

When it come to the point of intercourse, don't stop caressing him. Keep up your loveplay. Run your fingers through his hair, scratch his back and his buttocks, play with his anus and his balls. And don't just lie there silently while you're screwing: a few sexy and complimentary words can do an enormous amount to increase his excitement. Talk dirty to him: tell him how much you love him fucking you, tell him he has a beautiful hard cock and you love the feeling of it in your cunt.

And even when it's over, don't just lie there panting. Stroke and fondle him, squeeze his limp penis, and run your hands over his body. Kiss him and snuggle up to him. Tell him he's terrific.

When you've gotten to know him, loveplay doesn't have to be confined to the bedroom. Surprise him one evening by taking out his cock when he's watching television, and see if you can masturbate him to a climax. Feel up his ass when you're out shopping. Give him teasing kisses when nobody's looking. Physical love between a man and a woman is not something that starts and ends in a double bed—it's an ongoing relationship that should be kept ongoing by constant stimulation and titillation. The way some women shut their minds to loveplay once the orgasm is over makes you wonder whether they don't *like* sex.

And I'm sure that you do. . . .

# 9.

## *Coupling Up*

"Not a sound was heard, but the ottoman shook,
And my darling looked awfully worried,
As round her fair form I a firm hold took,
And John Thomas I silently buried."

—"The Burial of Sir John Thomas," anonymous, ca. 1880

Now that you're both well turned on, it's time for the Big Moment—intercourse.

The first time they have intercourse, most girls are disappointed. Come to that, most boys are disappointed, too. One woman I knew said that the first time she made love, she didn't even realize that the man had been inside her until afterward. Then she lay there thinking, Is that it? Is that all there is to it? The man, incidentally, was a very well-known film star, who made his name playing particularly virile roles.

Because the whole basis of intercourse is not much more than what an eighteenth-century French cynic called "the voluptuous friction of two intestines," it's easy for two lovers who don't know each other very well to find that, at first, they can't induce the right sort of friction at the right sort of pace. Different people's lovemaking rhythms vary quite considerably, and if you've been used to a man who keeps up a steady, plodding thrust throughout your coupling, another lover's uneven strokes and variations of speed could well throw you off.

Although it's not necessarily the most effective and most arousing position, the missionary position is probably best for the first time around—that is, you underneath and your lover on top. Because he's supporting his weight on his elbows, he has more freedom of hip and body movement, and you are almost completely free to wriggle about as you like.

When he climbs on top of you, it's nice gesture to take hold of his penis and guide it toward your vaginal entrance. At the same time you can make sure, if he has a foreskin, that it's well peeled back.

As he thrusts into you for the first time, try to move your hips to meet his at the deepest point of every stroke. That will stimulate you as much as it helps him, because his pubic bone will rub against your clitoris, and his penis will go even deeper into your vagina.

Quite a few women don't understand how much they can control the strength of their own erotic feelings during intercourse. If you want to feel him deeper inside you still, all you have to do is open your legs wider and raise them. His penis will then be sliding into you at a more acute angle and reach further. If you wrap your legs around his back and thrust yourself upwards every time he pushes in, you may even be able to feel the tip of his cock touching the neck of your womb. Ooh-eeh.

Don't forget your vaginal muscle exercises. When his penis is right up inside you, give him a rippling twitch and you'll increase his pleasure even more.

Intercourse can go on for as long as you want it to. Notice, I said as long as *you* want it to. Even though your lover may be feeling a frantic urge to come, you can slow down his feelings by parting your legs, so that there is less pressure on his penis from the walls of your vagina, and by completely relaxing your vaginal muscles. If you slow your hip movements to a gentle circular "grind," he will find it hard not to follow your example and slow down with you.

There is no reason at all why every act of intercourse should turn into a roller-coaster ride, starting off slow and then building up more and more speed until it's time for a whizzbang climax. You can start off slow, work up a little eroticism, then relax a while, change position, and start again. There's nothing to stop you changing position four or five times.

The only stipulation I would make is that when you're both near to climax, it's wise to adopt a position that's noted more for comfort than inventiveness. That way, you can control and enjoy the spasms of your orgasm to the fullest.

The reason that so much emphasis has been placed on love positions is because, until quite recently, the only way in which publishers could show pictures of people having intercourse was in the guise of "education." And so a whole spate of "educational" books came out showing the 456 variations of love. Actually, there are only about four or five really effective intercourse positions—that is, positions in which you can keep right on thrusting without spraining your left ankle or twisting your neck.

Here they are:

*Man on top, you underneath.* Despite the scorn accorded to this position by some sophisticated lovers, it has a lot going for it. Apart from the ease of control it gives to both partners' pelvic movements, it also enables you to kiss and caress face-to-face. The only disadvantage is that it's hard on the man's elbows, and it doesn't allow quite such deep penetration as some other positions.

*You on top, man underneath.* For you, this position is terrific. It means you can exercise very fine control over how deeply his penis goes into you (lean forward for less penetration, sit up straight for really deep insertion). You can also control the pace of your intercourse much more. If you're squatting on him, rather than lying with your legs straight out, his frenum will be highly stimulated against the back of your vagina, and this will add to his excitement. The disadvantages are that some men (although, fortunately, not so many these days) feel rather emasculated by having a woman on top of them calling the sexual tune, and that it can be tiring to your knees.

*You in front, man behind.* Sometimes known as "spoons," because you're lying together side-by-side like two spoons in a cutlery drawer, this position has the advantage of allowing deep penetration of his penis, and also giving his hands the freedom to fondle your breasts and clitoris from behind you. The main disadvantages are that you can't build up a very hot rhythm, because your hips are resting on the bed, and you can only kiss him over your shoulder.

*You on your back, man beside you.* This position (known as "scissors,") has the advantage of allowing you to kiss your lover more fully, while still giving him the opportunity to caress your breasts and clitoris. You lift your legs up, and he slides his cock in sideways. The unusual angle of entry gives him greater stimulation of the more sensitive parts of his penis, making up for the increased effort he has to make, under the weight of your legs and against the bed, to keep up a steadily mounting rhythm. The disadvantage here is that the cheeks of your ass tend to act as a buffer, making it more difficult for your lover to push himself in as deeply as he'd like.

Almost all other intercourse positions—whether they're sitting, standing, or lying down—are variations of these basic four. You can both use your imaginations to think of new ways of making love—he could sit on a chair, and you could lower yourself onto his lap—but to my mind, a whole repertoire of positions is not a vitally important part of good sex.

Variety comes in other, more exciting ways. From *where* you make love, and what you wear when you do it. From surroundings and atmosphere and surprises, rather than from technical adjustments to your legs, arms, and genitalia. I think it's far more important to be comfortable, so that you can concentrate on the sensations of his penis inside you, and his arms around you, and his kisses and words of passion rather than worrying about whether you're keeping up with the Joneses next door who have tried every position in the Kama Sutra *and* the one where you hang from the chandelier.

During intercourse, as we've seen, your lover's penis rubs against the inside of your vagina, a sensation that becomes increasingly pleasurable until his final ejaculation of sperm is triggered off. For you, it's the feeling of having a penis inside your vagina, and the pressures and rubbing on your clitoris, that eventually bring you off.

Most women grow quite flushed during intercourse, especially in the cheeks, and across the chest. Your breath, needless to say, comes in short pants, and your nipples will probably stiffen. Recent sexual research has shown that most women experience an erection of the nipples while they're having a climax, but it's not invariable or infallible. I've known women to have tremendous orgasms without a flicker of response from their nipples.

It's quite permissible, in fact it's rather nice, to stop in the middle of intercourse and have a rest and a little chat. If your lover tends to come slowly, or if he's wearing a condom, you may find that you *have* to, or else the poor guy will be exhausted by the time you get to a climax, and he won't enjoy himself one bit. Despite the way that many men and women perform, sexual intercourse isn't a race. Unless circumstances make it essential that you have a quick in-and-out fuck (you're doing it behind the filing cabinet, or he has a train to catch), then *take your time*.

I can never understand why most people have sex so quickly. You'd think they didn't enjoy it, the way they plunge in, thrash up and down, and then turn their backs on each other and go to sleep. You won't frustrate a man by stopping and relaxing, and running your fingers through his hair. In fact, when you resume operations, a man often feels an intensified sensation of pleasure in his penis.

What do you do if you're in the middle of intercourse and his cock starts going floppy? It's not your fault, so don't worry about that. He may have had a few too many Tom Collinses, or he may be anxious about something that has nothing to do with you. He may simply be tired.

Don't try to continue intercourse—move yourself away from him and pay some manual and oral attention to his penis. See if you can rub it into erection or lick it back into shape. Then, when it's hard again, guide it back to your vagina and recommence screwing. Whatever you do, don't sigh frustratedly or show any disappointment. You may in fact be disappointed, but the moment you let him know you feel that way, you might as well kiss the idea of any further erection good-bye.

If it keeps on flopping, regardless of your amatory manipulation, then gently give up for the time being. Kiss him, fondle his dangling dong, and then suggest that a few hours of sleep might restore him to his usual upstanding virility. "Floppy cock" is just one of those things that happen in sex, and you'll have to put up with it.

There are one or two variations on basic intercourse which are worth knowing about. In a lot of books on sex, you'll find them listed under "kinks" or "perversions," but so many people do them these days that they hardly merit that description at all.

The first is anal intercourse—that is, when the man inserts his penis into your anus. A lot of men like doing this, because the rectum is much tighter than the vagina, and they can get more powerful stimulation more quickly.

Anal intercourse is one of those things you have to *want* to do before it can be really successful. The muscles in your anus are tough and tight, and if you don't basically like the idea of what's going to happen, then they'll clam up like a sea anemone, and he'll find it next to impossible to push in his upstanding pecker. You have to re-e-e-lax.

As I said before, there's no need to worry that the inside of your ass is dirty. For as far as his penis can go, your rectum is usually empty of feces. But it does harbor very virulent bacteria, and it's vital that he doesn't insert his penis into your vagina after he's been screwing you up the ass. Otherwise, you could get an extremely uncomfortable infection. Similarly, he shouldn't put his finger in your vagina after probing your ass with it.

For anal intercourse, have on hand a tube of Johnson's KY, a clear odorless lubricant jelly which will ease the insertion of his penis. You should lie on your side with your legs bunched up, and "sit" on his erect penis. Don't let him force himself in too hard: the whole process should be slow and careful and gentle, because it will probably hurt you to begin with, and the muscles of the anus should not be forced.

Once he's inside, he can push himself back and forth with long, gentle strokes, and at the same time stimulate your clitoris and vagina with his free hand. Some men like to take a vibrator to bed when they have anal intercourse in mind, and push it up your vagina while they're ass-fucking you. The buzzing of the motor through the thin elastic wall between your rectum and vagina can give you both quite a stimulating thrill.

He will probably come inside your ass, but if you haven't taken any contraceptive precautions, be careful. The sperm can leak out of your anus while you sleep, and impregnate you. The result is what some cynics call "a backward child."

The morning after the night before, you will probably find that your ass is quite sore, but with practice, you'll discover that you can have anal intercourse without too much discomfort. Some women are extremely proud of the fact that their vaginas and their anuses are both versatile in lovemaking, and it certainly adds a new dimension to intercourse.

Then there's a second common variation—intercourse in the throat. I mention this because of the widespread popularity of Linda Lovelace's porn film *Deep Throat*, in which she was seen to take erect penises into her mouth right up to the hilt. Measure six inches back from your lips and you'll realize just how far down they went.

Linda Lovelace herself says that women who attempt to practice deep-throating without careful preparation for it can end up losing their dinner in a very prompt and spectacular way. This is because the penis, just like the handle of a spoon, triggers off the automatic gag reflex in the throat. If you want to vomit, just push your finger down your throat.

The penis also cuts off breathing, because it is so round and fat, and if you're a would-be Linda Lovelace, you'll have to learn to take gulps of air in between strokes of his cock, rather like a swimmer who trains herself to breathe whenever her face emerges from the water.

The trick of deep-throating is similar to the trick of sword-swallowing. The head must be held way back, so that the mouth and the throat form more or less a straight line. To achieve this, Linda Lovelace lies on her back on the bed and lets her head hang over the edge. Her lover then kneels on the floor in front of her, sliding his penis into her mouth and down her throat.

She recommends this technique to women who don't like the taste of sperm, because it all flushes down the throat without touching the taste buds in the mouth.

A warning: Linda Lovelace took a long time to develop her technique—first of all by putting her finger down her throat and learning not to gag, then by wiggling it about, and finally by gradually taking men's penises further and further in. If you don't train yourself this way, you could end up not only vomiting but with a damaged larynx. I hope I haven't put you off it too much.

While we're talking about oral intercourse, there's a spectacular trick that French prostitutes developed in the nineteenth century which became a favorite with many of their customers. It's called "the nose trick." When the man ejaculates his sperm into the woman's mouth, she sniffs it up inside her nose and blows it out through her nostrils, sometimes adding to the general amazement by catching it on her tongue. I wouldn't recommend it for a moment, but if you want to try ...

Finally, there's the arcane art of fist-fucking. This has caught on a great deal recently, particularly among homosexuals. The idea is that the man (or the woman) inserts his or her fist into either the vagina or the rectum of his or her partner. An American magazine reported that one man claimed, "I've been up to around the elbow."

"Must have been a really fat guy," the magazine asked him hopefully.

"No, no. In fact, he was one of the most beautiful little boys I've ever had. Went up so far I could feel the back of his rib cage from the inside. It was kind of scary, actually. After the initial slackness it all goes sort of ... hollow."

Enough, as the magazine said, to make a maggot gag.

I only mention this technique because some man may want to try it on you, and I strongly advise you to resist. It may be fashionable, but it's dangerous. The intestines could easily be damaged or infected, and no fad, however erotic, is worth major surgery.

There is usually no harm in any intercourse variation as long as you use common sense. You're old enough and beautiful enough not to let a man persuade you into doing something unequivocally stupid, no matter how sulky he may get, or how reasonable he may make it all sound. Respect your body and what sensations it can bring you, and your man will respect it too.

A question I'm often asked—by both men and women—is whether it's safe to have intercourse during your period. Some women actually feel more excited at that time of the month, but stay away from bedtime frolics because they're worried that (1) it might be unsafe, and (2) their lover won't like the sight of blood.

It is perfectly okay to have sex when you're menstruating, and some men actually get a kick out of it. The vagina is naturally much moister, and a little blood never did anyone any harm. If your lover goes pale and weak at the knees, don't force him to come to bed with you, but at the same time, remember that a sophisticated man will not consider it a valid excuse for opting out.

If your period is particularly heavy, a towel spread underneath you will prevent the sheets from being stained.

One of the initiation rites of certain chapters of the Hell's Angels is that a would-be biker has to have cunnilingus with a girl while she's menstruating, but this may not be a variation that your lover would particularly appreciate. Nonetheless, if he wants to, don't be embarrassed. Most men these days are quite unfazed by the idea of menstruation and accept it as the perfectly natural function that it is.

One thing, though—if you plan to have intercourse during your period, take out your tampon just before you get into bed and put it somewhere discreet. A friend of mind, a burly engineer, was quite upset when he climbed out of bed afterward and looked down at the floor. He thought he'd stepped on his girlfriend's pet white mouse, and killed it.

# 10.

## *Erotic Exercises*

"Her vigorous limbs are firm and fresh
And rich she blooms in prime of flesh.
This evening shall my bosom prove
The richest ecstasies of love."
    —"Before," anonymous, 19th century

As a woman, sexual intercourse is one of the most intensely strenuous physical activities you're ever likely to perform, with the exception of childbirth. And one thing kind of follows the other, doesn't it?

But while great emphasis is placed these days on exercising in preparation for giving birth, no emphasis at all is placed on exercising for sex. The energy you use during one act of love could fuel you over a 220-yard sprint, and yet you wouldn't expect to run like that successfully without any kind of training at all.

You can enjoy sex much more if you're basically fit. When you're perspiring and panting and out of breath, you're not going to enjoy your orgasms so much, and you're not going to feel anything but exhausted after it's all over. To be terrific in bed, you need stamina and strength—you need too be sound in wind and limb.

The exercises that follow are designed to bring you, over the period of a month, into a reasonable physical condition for good lovemaking. They will enable you to move your pelvis more robustly, support your own weight during intercourse without tiring, and generally keep you in good fighting trim. There won't be so much of the "not tonight, darling, I'm too tired."

Like all exercises, these will only help you if you keep on doing them. Set aside ten minutes in the morning or evening *every day*, and keep at them. It'll help, too, if you give up smoking. Not only will your breath and your hair smell better to the man you love, you'll be able to keep up the pace of sex without gasping for air.

## Week One

1. Stand with your legs slightly apart and your hands on your hips. Now bend forward and touch your toes. Don't worry about keeping your knees straight. (10 times)

2. Lie on your stomach on the floor with your arms flat against your sides. Lift your head as far from the floor as you can, and then lower it again. (10 times)

3. Lie on your back on the floor, lifting your buttocks clear of the carpet by supporting your hips with your hands. Start "cycling" with your legs in the air as slowly as you can. (25 cycles)

4. Lie on your back on the floor. Then sit up, and without help from your hands and arms, lean forward and touch your toes. (10 times)

## Week Two

1. Stand with your legs slightly apart and your hands on your hips. Now bend forward and touch your toes without bending your legs. (10 times)

2. Lie on your stomach on the floor with your arms flat against your sides. Now raise your head and your legs as far off the floor as you can, then lower them again. (10 times)

3. Stand with your legs together and your hands on your hips. Keeping your back vertical, and without taking your hands off your hips, squat down slowly, then stand up again. (10 times)

4. Lie on your back on the floor and cycle (30 cycles)

5. Stand with ycur hands on your hips and your feet apart. Now lean to the right, from your waist upwards. Then return to standing straight. Now lean to the left, from the waist upwards. (20 times)

## Week Three

1. Stand with your legs slightly apart and your hands on your hips. Now bend forward and touch your left toe without bending your knees, then return to an upright position. Then bend forward and touch the floor in be-

tween your feet, then return to upright. Finally bend forward and touch your right toe. (20 times)

2. Lie on your stomach on the floor with your arms flat against your sides. Now raise your head and your legs as far as you can, and also lift your arms up behind you as far as possible. (15 times)

3. Run on the spot, keeping count each time your left foot touches the floor. After every 10 paces, squat down with your hands on your hips and your back straight. (40 paces)

4. Lie on your back on the floor. Sit up, without using your arms or hands, and reach forward to touch your toes. (20 times)

5. Stand with your hands on your hips and your feet apart. Rotate your upper body around as far as you can from the waist. (15 rotations)

## Week Four

1. Stand with your legs slightly apart and your hands on your hips. Bend forward and touch your left toe, then bend forward and touch the floor, then your right toe. Each time you bend forward to touch your toes, give a little double "bounce." (25 times)

2. Lie on your stomach on the floor with your arms flat against your sides. Raise your head as far as you can, then lift your arms backwards and upwards as high as possible. (20 times)

3. Run on the spot, squatting down every 10 paces. (50 paces)

4. Lie on your back on the floor. Sit up, without using your arms or hands, and reach forward to touch your toes. (20 times)

5. Stand with your hands on your hips and your feet apart. Rotate your body from the waist.  (25 rotations)

# 11.

## *Be Your Own Sex Therapist*

You've probably realized by now that there's more to the *practical* side of women's liberation than knowing how to wire a plug, change a flat tire, or wallpaper your own apartment.

But have you thought just how much you, as a liberated woman, can do to help your lover out of his sexual problems?

"Who *me?* What the hell can *I* do about a limp penis?"

The truth is that you can do *plenty*. So much, in fact, that Masters & Johnson, those indomitable sex researchers from St. Louis, Missouri, considered the role played by the female partner to be an essential ingredient in effective therapy for several of the more common erotic ailments.

In Chapter 6, I talked briefly about ways in which you can help your lover's occasional failures to keep his erection, and what to do if he ejaculates prematurely. These conditions are pretty easy to handle if they're caused by a temporary anxiety, or a temporary illness, or a temporary intake of six very dry martinis.

But supposing the symptoms persist, and supposing they even get worse? Suddenly you have a dearly beloved man on your hands, but he's unable to provide you with the very service you desired him for. It's like having a wonderfully expensive stereo set that does everything except play records.

When a situation like this arises (or descends, rather), you need to sit by yourself with a generous measure of your favorite liquor and have a think. This think-session must be quite cold-blooded, but many men have the same kind of thoughts about women, and so you mustn't feel guilty about doing it. Or not *too* guilty, anyway.

If your lover is consistently failing to satisfy you sexually, and you *know* that the fault is not in you but in him, you will have to decide whether you want to stay with him or not. If you love him principally for his cock, and you don't think too much of the surrounding man, then you may well decide that his Time Has Come, and that he must go and Never Again Darken Your Doorstep, let alone your bed. Satisfaction or separation.

But if there's more too your lover than a desirable dong, you may well decide you want to stay with him. But if you want to stay, you'll have to appreciate what the terms are. So, too, must he, and when you've finished thinking this all over, you'll have to tell him. The terms are simply these: that if you stay together, you'll have to work together to overcome his sexual problems.

Your help, however, must be wholeheartedly, freely, and generously given, with no trace of frustration, sarcasm, annoyance, or impatience. If you think you're going to have any of these feelings, then you'd be better off splitting up, because home sex therapy is very hard work, very trying on the sexual nerves, and very abrasive to your relationship.

When you decide to help your man over his sex problems, whether he's your husband or your regular lover or just a guy you feel a lot for, then you have to be prepared, for as long as the treatment lasts, to be unselfish and generous and constantly *giving*. It's worth your understanding that you can make the difference between a man being a great lover and a sexual dud. You hold that power in your hands (and in your vagina), and it's up to you whether you use it or not.

This is the experience of Rita, 25: "When Carl and I started to try and do something about his impotence, I don't think either of us had any idea how difficult and exhausting the whole thing was going to be. I'm not sure whether I would have even tried if I'd known what the treatment would take out of me. I used to lie in bed at night, in the dark, with Carl lying asleep beside me, and I used to stare at the dark ceiling and huge fat tears would roll out of my eyes. I used to pray God to help us, because it didn't seem like anyone else could or would. I went to my doctor, and he said to me, 'Are you married?' When I said I wasn't, he just shrugged and said, 'Then you don't have a problem, do you?' I knew that Masters and Johnson were into sex therapy, but they can't help everyone in the world, and who the hell can spend weeks and weeks in St. Louis?"

The most common of all male sexual problems, as we've talked about earlier, is premature ejaculation. This means that your lover comes to a climax almost as soon as he has inserted his penis into you. Most therapists define "premature ejaculation" as a climax that comes to the boil before his penis has been inside you for more than thirty seconds, which is the same time-span as a television commercial. Masters and Johnson, more sensibly and more humanely, define the condition as your lover's inability to hold back his climax long enough for you to have an orgasm at least 50 percent of the time. In other words, *your* orgasmic expectations must be reasonable, but *his* target for improvement should be geared to *your* satisfaction, rather than to an arbitrary time-span. It's no use saying, "Let's try and hold it back for just one more commercial, Harry." As long as he holds it back in time for you to make it over the top, that's fine.

Why do men suffer from premature ejaculation? As I said before, it's a nervous habit. It usually dates from your lover's early sexual experiences, when his susceptibility to ejaculation was much greater, and when he was encouraged to reach a climax as fast as possible—either by an impatient hooker or by the circumstances of making love to teen-age girlfriends on their parents' couch, with Mom's returning footsteps coming up the path. Shoot now, or forever hold your piece.

It is also associated with men who have been brought up to believe (or who have never been disabused of the belief) in sexual chauvinism. There are still millions of men—*millions*—in the United States today who believe that sexual intercourse is primarly for the satisfaction of the man. Whether the woman has an orgasm or not doesn't even enter their heads. Many don't even know that a woman is capable of having an orgasm.

The result is that they ejaculate quickly for their own release, leaving their wives or girlfriends aroused but unfulfilled. Understandably, the woman becomes hostile to sex because it always leaves her frustrated, and the sexual relationship decays rapidly. The man begins to question his own sexual ability to the point where he may even become impotent, making the situation doubly impossible.

If your lover ejaculates prematurely, there is a considerable hope that he can be cured of his problem. By today's newest techniques, it is one of the easiest of sex difficulties to overcome.

But first of all, you'll have to sit down with him and explain that you're not satisfied with his lovemaking, and that both of you are going to have to work hard toward improving it. If he doesn't even know that you're supposed to have an orgasm, it's time he did—so tell him. Don't be all militant and furious about it, or he'll walk straight out of the door and you won't have anybody to be therapeutic *with*. Don't *blame* him. He may have been insensitive to your sexual needs in the past, but you're giving him a chance to improve himself, and that's all that matters. As one divorce lawyer recently told me, "There are two words that ought to be rubbed out of the language. 'Fault' is one, and 'blame' is the other."

When you start work on your lover as a home sex

therapist, you will require one quality above all others: patience.

Learn to hold back your frustration when things keep going wrong. Learn to explain to your lover, in calm clear words, just where he's going wrong, and what he can do about it. There may be times when he loses *his* temper and rants and rages at you, but that will only be his own self-criticism and humiliation boiling over. Stay cool. Be patient.

Start your therapy by lying naked on your bed with your lover and doing what sex therapists call "pleasuring" each other. There is to be no intercourse during these sessions, and no ejaculation. The purpose of the procedure is for both of you to refamiliarize yourselves with the things that turn you on, and to give pleasure to your partner. *Give* is the important word. Show your lover how to give you a good time—by kissing you and caressing you and stimulating your clitoris and vagina—without worrying about his own enjoyment. Then do the same to him, underlining the fact that sex is never a one-way street.

After a week or so of pleasure sessions, you're ready to begin the premature ejaculation technique. To do this effectively, you have to know how to grip your lover's penis in such a way that you can curb his urge to ejaculate.

You do this by placing the ball of your thumb just under the opening in the head of his penis, and then placing your first and second fingers around the shaft, one on top of the ridge around the head of his penis, and one below. You may have to try a few times to get the grip exactly right, but once you do, you'll know you're doing it correctly. This is because when you *squeeze* your lover's penis in this way, he will lose the urge to ejaculate. Nobody knows why this happens, but it does. You can squeeze as hard as you like, because you'd have to be Wonderwoman to hurt his erect penis in this way.

You will both have to *talk* while you're undergoing

this treatment, because it is vital for your lover to tell you when he feels the urge to climax.

Once you have learned to control his ejaculation in this way, you can start to have intercourse again. At first, your lover should lie on his back, and you should lie on top of him, lowering yourself gently onto his erect cock. The first couple of times, don't move at all. Just let him get used to the idea of having his penis inside you without feeling the need to ejaculate at once. If the urge wells up in him at any time, simply lift yourself off him, apply the *squeeze,* and reinsert.

When you've mastered this, you're ready for a little bit of movement. With his penis inside you, it's natural for you to want to move his penis in and out, stimulating yourself to orgasm—particularly if you haven't had satisfactory sex in a long time. The trouble is, if you did this now, you would overstimulate your lover's penis and bring him to another quick climax.

So, to get over this difficulty, have him arouse you almost to orgasm *before* you start intercourse—with his tongue or his fingers or whatever he likes. A vibrator is always handy for titillation of this kind, if you have one.

When you start intercourse, you will be almost on the verge of a climax anyway, so it won't be hard for him to hold his ejaculation back long enough to satisfy you.

It takes anything from six months to a year for couples to learn ejaculation control, but the success rate of the technique has been incredibly high. Many lovers find that they have to give up the man-on-top intercourse position, because it is harder to control ejaculation in this position than any other. But girl-on-top, side-by-side, and other positions are equally satisfying—particularly when they're a positive help to better lovemaking.

After premature ejaculation, the most common male sexual problem is *impotence*. This is a very much more serious and complex problem, but there are ways in which you, as a man's lover, can help him to find his way back to sexual virility.

It's important to know *why* he's impotent. Anxiety, as

we've seen, is a frequent cause of impotence, and even anxiety about the possibility of being impotent can cause impotence. If the anxiety situation is temporary, though, the impotence will probably be temporary—provided you don't make your lover feel inadequate and feeble.

But what if the cause is even more deeply rooted than that? Some men—and these are the hardest of all to cure—are impotent because they have rigid religious beliefs about the wickedness and uncleanliness of sex. Another hard-core group, as far as therapy is concerned, are homosexuals, or men with some homosexual tendencies. But don't immediately leap to the conclusion that your lover is a gay religious fanatic. There are plenty of other, more common reasons why men become impotent.

The hasty hooker is sometimes to blame, if your lover's early sex experiences involved prostitutes. She may have mocked his performance in bed, and that could well have caused him to believe that he wasn't any good at sex and couldn't satisfy women. Sometimes a boy's mother makes sexual advances to him, and that can give him traumatic feelings about intercourse—depending on the mother, of course.

Premature ejaculation, as we've just seen, can cause impotence, and so can overindulgent drinking and drugtaking. We've discussed how to tackle premature ejaculation, but it's also worth remembering that even when heavy drinking and drug-taking are given up, the impotence may linger on for a while.

The best thing that you can ever do for an impotent man is to make him understand that he doesn't have to do anything to attain—and keep—his erection. He doesn't have to furrow his brow, clench his fists, strain his ass, or anything. Watching an impotent man trying to hold on to a fading erection is like watching someone trying to stop a balloon leaking by glaring at it.

The way in which you can help to restore your man's confidence in his sexual ability is by, first of all, clearing your mind of any resentment or bitchiness you've felt about him because he hasn't been doing his duty as a lover and a phallic symbol.

You will never get anywhere with curing his impotence if you resent his inability and show that you resent it.

The next thing to do is have a few more sessions of "pleasuring." With the home treament of impotence, you must have some pretty firm rules about these sessions. *There is to be no intercourse for six weeks.* That has to be the rule, and you both have to stick to it. It seems frustrating, but it has its logic. It is vital for your lover to feel that he has no duty to perform when he has an erection. He is only there to fondle and be fondled, to suck and be sucked, to grope and be groped. Keep on touching and stroking him, even when he's limp as a wet dish towel, and don't even stop to think whether he's hard or soft.

Once he has learned, deep down inside that brain of his, that he has no *obligation* to produce a hard-on, he will find it easier to keep his penis up. This is a mental knack that, for men who've been chronically impotent, is difficult to acquire. It's like the situation in *Tom and Jerry*, when Jerry runs off a cliff top and stays safely up in the air until he looks down and realizes he's a hundred feet above the ground. Even when your lover is able to produce a good and sound erection, there will still be moments when he looks down and realized he's a hundred feet above the earth, and his hard-on, like Jerry, drops rapidly to ground zero.

If your lover has a severe psychological hangup, then he will obviously have to seek assistance from a qualified therapist. But your calming influence and your "pleasuring" sessions will still constitute an important part of his convalescence. He doesn't have to produce an erection for his therapist, after all—he has to produce it for *you*.

Treating impotence is a frustrating, lengthy, and often disappointing procedure. If you love your lover enough, though, you'll give it a try. You will be just as much a winner as he, if it all turns out for the best.

Another—less common—sex ailment is an inability to

reach a climax, known in the trade as "ejaculatory in-competence." There's a good old home remedy for this, and it's worth trying as soon as possible, because ejacula-tory incompetence can sometimes lead to impotence.

Men suffer from an inability to ejaculate for several reasons. Usually, they have some kind of phobia about women and their vaginas. Masters and Johnson recorded the case of a young Jewish boy who was put off by reli-gious teachings about the uncleanliness of women dur-ing their monthly period. Another man's inability dated from the day he had returned home from work to discover his wife in bed with a stranger—whose freshly shot semen was seeping from his wife's vagina. He was never able to ejaculate into his wife again.

The treatment for ejaculatory incompetence is comparatively simple, but again it takes *patience*. The trick is to masturbate your lover by hand until he is on the verge of ejaculation, and then insert his penis into your vagina. Once he has actually managed to ejaculate inside you, he will find it easier and easier to come to a normal climax. Masters and Johnson treated their pa-tients with a fairly high degree of success, and unless your lover is a religious freak or a psychotic misogynist, you shouldn't have much trouble in persuading him to come inside you.

I'm not going to pretend for one minute that it's easy to be your own sex therapist. It isn't. It's tough and it's frustrating, and you may find it very difficult to over-come the built-in resistance and sexual ego of your lover. You may find, even after you've done your best to help your lover with a sex problem, that on your own you're incapable of doing enough.

But if you know that you're capable of helping, and that sex difficulties such as premature ejaculation and impotence are capable of being cured, you will be in a much better position to help your lover out of his erotic nose-dive.

# 12.

## *How Important Is Your Orgasm?*

Today's lovers still haven't quite come to terms with the female orgasm. It's been known to exist for a long time, but the proprieties of midde-class Victorian thinking did not admit that ladies could actually enjoy sex. "Shut your eyes," was the classic advice from a mother to her daughter on the night before the wedding, "and think of England."

Once publicly admitted, however, the female orgasm became more and more complicated with every passing year. First there was the controversy about vaginal and clitoral orgasms, which, as we've seen, was all nonsense. But then Masters and Johnson, the St. Louis sex researchers, announced that women could have orgasm after orgasm until they collapsed from exhaustion, and that the female sexual capacity, as far as they could make out, was almost infinite.

Imagine the traumatic shudder that went through men, with their one-shot equipment, on hearing that women were technically insatiable!

Of course, there's a big difference between being technically insatiable and finding real satisfaction. And even though many women are capable of experiencing and enjoying multiple orgasms, most are satisfied with one good one.

There are times when you will feel satisfied after having had no orgasm at all. But I think it's important that you make your lover realize that his part in lovemaking is to help to bring you to a climax. It will make him work harder, and it will improve his technique; and both of you stand to gain from benefits like that. If you never insist on having an orgasm, he will rarely insist on giving you one, and your affair will choke itself on his laziness and your frustration.

But how do you insist? If a man has made love to you, and had his ejaculation, and is now quite contentedly preparing himself for a good night's sleep, what on earth can you do to make him bring you off?

Well, you may not get much change out of his penis. You can try, though, by rubbing it vigorously and hard, and maybe sucking the end of it at the same time. But if his prick insists on remaining floppy and inert, your lover should still be capable of giving you the climax you desire.

Take his hand, press it between your legs, on your clitoris, and have him start masturbating you. You don't have to say a word, and he'll get the message. If he can't quite find your most sensational spot, guide him to it, and adjust the rhythm of his rubbing to the pace you most prefer by holding his hand and showing him.

If you want him to lick you to orgasm, ask him by whispering, "Lick me" in his ear. You'll find that once his face is between your thighs, you can exercise quite a lot of control over the stimulation he gives you. Press his nose and mouth into your vulva, rub your clitoris against his hair, and *use* his head and face as an instrument of erotic arousal. It will turn him on as well, since most men have a little of the masochist in them, and you may be treated to a re-starched penis.

When you actually have your orgasm, tell him what it's like. Some men seem to believe that it's nothing more than a quiet muscular wince, while others expect the fourth of July to come bursting out of your ears. Good sex is always founded on good communication between lovers, and if he knows what your orgasm feels like, then he can identify more with your experience when he's making love to you.

There is no reason why any woman today should put up with unsatisfying sex from her lover or husband, provided he's medically fit. But frequently it will take initiative on your part to make your man understand that you need to have an orgasm, and that he ought to be giving it to you.

Tracey, a 29-year-old secretary, told me how she cured her lover's sex-laziness forever:

"He knew about female orgasm in theory, but he never did anything about it in practice. As long as he'd shot his wad, then he was happy. He didn't seem to consider my feelings at all. So I started buying magazines like *Playgirl* and leaving them around the apartment. That made him jealous and angry. Then, one night after we'd had sex, or rather *he'd* had sex, I started masturbating. I did it quite openly and made a lot of panting noises and moans. He was half asleep at first, but then he turned around as though someone had fired a catapult up his ass, and shouted, 'What the fuck are *you* doing?' I said I was trying to have an orgasm, because he never gave me one. He was very upset, but mainly because I'd humiliated him and shown him up. 'How did I know you even wanted one?' he yelled at me. But in the end he calmed down, and after that I never had any trouble with him at all. He always made sure that I came. You see, I think he appreciated something: that despite the fact he hadn't been satisfying me properly, I hadn't gone off hunting for another man. I think men could do the same thing to women who weren't very good in bed: they could leave copies of *Playboy* around, and jerk themselves off in front of their wives or girlfriends or whatever. That really pricks someone's conscience."

Is it necessary to have simultaneous orgasms? That is, do you and your lover have to come together to make really satisfying love?

Well, it's nice if it happens once in a while, because both of your climaxes can be improved by the muscular spasms going on in each other's bodies when you're coming. Many women find their orgasms are actually triggered off by the sensation of their lover's sperm spurting against the cervix. And many men are brought to ejaculation by the rippling sensation inside a woman's vagina when she comes.

As you grow more used to the technique and rhythms that your lover uses, you'll find it easier to experience simultaneous orgasm. You'll be able to tell by the hardening of his cock and the tightening of his balls when he's about to ejaculate, just as he can tell by the stiffening of your nipples and the feelings inside your cunt when you're on the point of orgasm.

But simultaneous orgasm isn't *essential* to good lovemaking, and you mustn't be disappointed if it doesn't happen. Just because one of you has climaxed, that doesn't mean that the party is suddenly over. It can go on and be just as sexy, with one of you trying to bring the other to a satisfying finish.

What happens if you find you're unable to have an orgasm? If, no matter how hard you try, you just can't seem to get to the summit when you're making love?

This is a very common female sex problem. You're not at all unusual. There are usually two principal reasons for it, both of which are easily cured. First, you're not relaxed enough. You're trying too hard to reach a climax, and because of that, it's eluding you. You're suffering from the same debilitating anxiety that causes a man's penis to flop.

Secondly, your lover may not be caressing you and stimulating you properly, and he may be coming too quickly for you.

To get over the first problem, try taking a tranquilizer an hour or two before bedtime (a hefty-sized drink will also do), and do everything you can to relax when your lover starts making love to you. Don't *worry* about reaching a climax. You can't help it along by tensing your muscles and furrowing your brow. It will come because your nerves have been sufficiently stimulated, and it will come by itself. Join your lover in having sex, and forget about it until it creeps up and hits you over the head.

The second problem is, admittedly, a little more tricky. If your lover isn't turning you on enough, then try resisting his first attempts to push in his penis. Make him fight for it—and caress you more—before you part your legs for him. But explain what you're doing or he might think you just don't feel like it tonight, and quit in a huff. Say, "Suck my breasts first, darling ..." or "Rub me with your fingers before you put it in ..." or something like that.

If he's coming too quickly for you, then we've already seen what to do about that.

You can take advantage of your female capacity for having more than one orgasm by *not waiting* until your lover is ready for his ejaculation and having a climax as soon as you feel like it. You can then have another when he's nearing his own. It won't particularly matter if your first orgasm sends him over the top, because you'll still be reasonably satisfied.

There's nothing mysterious or weird about the female orgasm, even though some women have them more readily than others. Almost every woman is capable of having a climax, and what's more she *ought* to be having it. Of course it's possible to put up with sex in which you don't have an orgasm—many women have tolerated it for years—but it will lead to all kinds of unhappy erosions of your relationship with your lover. Your frustration may not show itself as anger against him, but it will come out in other ways.

If you've tried longer and more intensive loveplay, if you've tried tranquilizers and desensitizers and everything else and you still can't reach an orgasm, go and talk to your doctor. It's that important. He may be able to suggest some ways of helping you, or he may put you in touch with a psychiatrist. Many women are unable to have satisfactory sex because of repressive sexual behavior in their families when they were young, and it does take professional assistance to sort out a problem like that.

A woman who has regular orgasms is a sexually happy woman, and only a sexually happy woman can drive a man wild in bed. Make sure you're getting *yours* regularly.

# 13.

## *Beside the Lake,*
## *Beneath the Trees*

"I persuaded her to stand by the gate. She hid her face in her hands on the top rail, as I slowly raised her dress; what glories were unfolded to view, my prick's stiffness was renewed in an instant at the sight of her delicious buttocks, so beautifully relieved by the white of her pretty drawers. I stood up and prepared to take possession of the seat of love—when, alas! a sudden shriek from Annie, and her clothes dropped. A bull had unexpectedly appeared on the other side of the gate, and frightened my love by the sudden application of his cold, damp nose to her forehead."
—"Sport Among the She-Noodles," ca. 1870

*Where* you make love is almost as important as *how* you make love. It can sometimes be just as important as *to whom* you make love.

Sex is a sensual experience, and sensuality is heightened when all your perceptive faculties are aroused. Not just genitals, and the lips, and maybe the nipples, but the whole body. And if you're able to make love in the kind of setting that stirs the senses of sight and smell and hearing as well, then so much the better.

I'm not decrying sex in the bedroom. There can be times when plunging into a clean, fresh bed with the man you love can be the warmest and most exciting thing you can do. And, let's face it, most of us, most of the time, have sexual intercourse in bed in the evening, and don't believe any one who tells you otherwise. Having sex in bed is nothing to be ashamed of.

But every now and then, it adds piquancy to your love life if you can have sex in a different place. It might be uncomfortable and hurried, but the sheer eroticism of having intercourse with the man you love in the back seat of his car, or behind an open door at someone's party, or just out of sight of a clambake crowd behind a sand dune, is worth almost any inconvenience you can think of.

You will really turn on the man you love—and take, if not one small step for mankind, then one giant step toward total eroticism—if you show him that you're ready for sex at unusual times. Here's an example from Birgitta, a 22-year-old Swedish secretary:

"It was winter, and my boyfriend Henry and I were staying near Uppsala. The snow was very thick and deep, although the sky was clear. Just about midday, we went out to shoot rabbits. We were both dressed up in our fur coats and boots of course. The woods were beautiful and quiet and clear.

"When we had been walking for a little while, kissing and laughing, I said to Henry that he ought to feel inside my coat. We rested up against a tree, and he took off his glove and put his hand inside my coat. I was wearing long woollen stockings, red ones, that came right up to my thighs, but I had left off my panties, and so under my woollen dress, between my legs, I was quite bare. Henry felt me there, and put his fingers up my pussy, and rubbed me until I was very worked up.

"Then he opened his coat, which is a big silver fox, and wrapped it around us both. Then he unzipped his trousers, and pushed his cock into me. We fucked like that, standing by that tree in the middle of all the snow, and I can remember how our breath froze on our hair. We had a climax almost together, and when we walked back, his come kept sliding out of me and freezing down the legs of my stockings."

Making love like that is not as comfortable as having

it in the privacy and warmth of your own bedroom, but it's that kind of experience that makes an affair *memorable*. And if you want to be memorable, if you want to be the kind of woman that he never forgets for the rest of his life, then that's the kind of variety that will insure you a niche in his sexual hall of fame.

Here's another example, seen through the colored glasses of male sexual fantasy, from my friend Jan Cremer, author of the notorious autobiography *I, Jan Cremer*:

I opened the door and walked into a tremendous, mirror-covered bathroom. It suddenly dawned on me that I wasn't alone. Miss Judith, the dancer, was staring at me. "Excuse me," I mumbled. I wanted to get out of there but I couldn't seem to move from the spot. Judith, who was combing her hair, didn't look the least surprised to see me there. "Are you coming or going, honey," she said. My heart and my cock jumped up at the same moment. "Coming, if that's OK with you," I managed to say. She made it obvious that it was fine with her, this vampire-woman I'd been eyeing all evening. I got excited just looking at her, with her green fingernails, green lips, and green eyes.

I don't remember who made the first move, but suddenly we were up against the wall, she with her back to it and me glued to her body, both of us wriggling and writhing and breathing hard. Then I was inside her skirt and she was inside my pants and we fell on to a straw mat on the tiled floor. Her face glowed with a witch's ecstasy and she shoved and wiggled underneath me, moving my cock up and down with one hand and running the green fingernails of the other up and down my back.

I pulled up her leopard-skin dress, pulled down her damp panties and rammed my hard tool into her. We rose and fell on the hard floor until we came together, with a shout. We stood up. She pulled her panties off over her high-heeled shoes with practiced efficiency, and used them to wipe come from between her legs, finally stowing them in her handbag. "It was marvellous," she said.

Now Jan Cremer is given to lusty exaggeration, and his book was written to shock. But many men will recognize in that scene the kind of sexual fantasy they have often had: taking a willing woman in an exciting and unlikely spot. I'm not suggesting that you have to go around with green fingernails and act like a whore, but if you show more than a slight inclination to indulge your lover's erotic daydreams, you'll probably be doing more to please him than any woman he's ever had before.

Sex in unusual locations can roughly be divided into two different types, although obviously they will often overlap. First is the planned expedition to find somewhere great and outdoorsy to make love. Second is the quick, unpremeditated screw in places where discovery is an imminent peril.

There are few sensations quite as erotic as taking all your clothes off on the beach or in the woods and lying under the sun making love. But an idyll like that has to be carefully worked out beforehand. If your lover doesn't know any good spots, don't just pile into the car and go hunting, because you'll both end up growing more and more frustrated, and if you do find a place, it will more than likely be awkward and uncomfortable, and rainclouds will have suddenly moved in from the sea.

Keep an eye open for possible places when you go on weekend drives. When you discover somewhere, check it out carefully. If it's a field of wheat, make sure that by the time you revisit it, it won't have been turned into stubble by combine harvesters. If it's a wood or a field or an orchard, check that it isn't the kind of private property that's likely to be patrolled by game wardens. One couple I knew made love in a forest in Montana, only to realize afterwards that they had been meticulously observed by a fire warden from a nearby tower.

"If I'd had the energy," said the man, "I would have climbed the tower and decked him."

Take simple food with you on your love safari—wine, cheese, bread. Take a big comfortable blanket. Grass may look soft, but when your naked back is being pressed against it by the weight of an amorous swain, you'll suddenly realize just how many stones and prickles and lumps there are in it. Don't forget the anti-mosquito spray, either. A love bite on the breast is one thing; a wasp sting is definitely another.

All these precautions and preparations may sound like a drag, but the ultimate lovemaking is worth it. We've grown so urbanized that we rarely get to taste the pleasure of nakedness in the outdoors, and many couples I know have found that the delights of sex under the sky have worked wonders for them.

"I guess it's kind of ridiculous to say we felt like Adam and Eve," says 24-year-old Millie, a public relations executive. "But when Steve and I went out into the woods on a visit to Pennsylvania, and stripped down and made love, it was just as if we were children of nature. Steve looked beautiful, running around naked. He looked more of a man and yet more of a boy as well. And when we were actually making it, and I could feel the sun shining on my back and the wind blowing around between our legs, that was so fantastic that I wondered if I'd ever be satisfied with making it indoors again."

If your lover seems disinclined to try this kind of sexual variety, do your best to push him into it. Organize it all for him, if necessary. Men can grow lazy about where and how they have sex, and it might all seem like too much of an effort for him. But when it happens, he will really appreciate it. The great thing about the outdoors is that it's romantic as well as erotic, and if he's ever had any doubts about how much he loves you, a beautiful session in the woods will do a great deal to dispel them.

The other type of unusual sex—having it where and when the urge takes you—is rarely romantic, but it's certainly erotic. The fear of being discovered as you rapidly accomplish your act of love will send the adrenalin throbbing through your veins, heightening your sensitivity and your sexual pleasure. Remember, though, that while you can expect some truly remarkable excitement, you must also be prepared for failure. The anxiety may get to your lover's erection and cause him to suffer instant droop. You may be interrupted halfway through by someone knocking on the door or walking into the room. The position you're in may be so uncomfortable that one or the other of you is unable to reach a climax.

But it's enough, as far as your lover is concerned, that you have the hots for him so strongly that you wanted to *try*. Even if you can't quite make it, the memory of doing it will provide you both with an enticing erotic fantasy that you can relive in the privacy of your bedroom.

Jackie, 25, had sex with her lover Jason, 27, in a well-known New York art gallery:

"The whole place was practically empty. We wandered around looking at the paintings and then came to a small room that was off one of the main galleries. There was a security man in the main room, but I think he was almost asleep. We were both footsore, so we sat down on the couch in this small room and talked for a while, and then Jason started to grow amorous, and kiss me, and squeeze my breasts through my dress. I began to get really excited, and I fondled his cock through the pocket of his pants, until I felt it grow hard.

"I pulled my tights and panties down and then knelt on all fours on the couch, with my bare bottom in the air and my dress pulled up. Jason opened his pants and knelt behind me, and pushed in his cock. We had to do it very quietly, or the security guy would've come along to see what the hell we were doing. I could hear people walking around the main gallery, too, and somebody only had to walk down our way to see everything. But that was what made it so thrilling.

"I don't think we've ever made love so quickly. We thrust and thrust and thrust, and we both came, not together, but almost together. Then I quickly pulled up my tights and panties again, and Jason did up his pants, and we went on walking round the gallery. But all the time I could smell the sex we'd just had, and when we looked in the mirror in the entrance hall, we both looked rudely and vulgarly healthy."

You can make love anywhere, or almost anywhere. One of the newer fads is for having intercourse on an aircraft, a feat which will make you automatically a member of the "mile-high" club. The best time to do it is during a night flight, when the movies are being shown, and you can conceal your erotic activities under an airline blanket. Unlike a bus or a train, if they discover what you're doing, they can't very well throw you off.

For those who don't fly—united, or otherwise—there is another new game—elevator sex. The rules of the game are simple: How much can you manage, sexwise, before the elevator reaches its destination? Janie, a 19-year-old stenographer for a Chicago law firm, told me: "It's better when the elevator's crowded. My boyfriend and I went up to the restaurant on top of the John Hancock building—that's ninety-five floors. The elevator was packed, and we stood at the back. David stood behind me, and lifted my skirt, and fondled me all the way up to the roof. He was turning me on so much I had to bite my lips to keep quiet. Nobody even noticed. In elevators, everybody stands facing the door, so if you're standing at the back, it's as good as being in the back row at the movies."

It might seem like teen-age stuff, but the movies have still got a lot going for them as far as surreptitious petting is concerned. You might like to upgrade the activity, however, by trying it at a classical concert. Nobody expects you to be caressing your lover's penis during Schubert's Fantasy in C, and the secret of sex like that is to do it when it's the last possible thing that would enter people's minds.

A publisher friend of mine was caressed by his mistress's bare foot under the table of a ritzy restaurant (don't try it at hamburger joints—they don't have long tableclothes). An advertising copywriter was succulently fellated by his secretary while he continued to type. His

work came out something like: gfsxcz jghruy kfhfj
ooooohhhhhh.

Maybe a doubt enters your mind when you think
about doing things like this. Why, you're thinking,
should I behave like a whore?

The answer is: you won't be. By thinking more
creatively about sex, and by expressing your physical
feelings for your lover more readily, you will be doing a
great deal to help yourself put your erotic feelings into
perspective. Sex is by no means the only ingredient in a
successful affair, but it will assume unnatural pro-
portions if it's reserved for special occasions, if it's allowed to become a ritual. If you only ever make love in
bed in the evening, then your lover will grow to expect
that every evening he takes you out, you're going to
make love. Sex will become a routine, and there are few
things more whoreish than that.

Whores have sex on demand—a man's demand. They
also have sex in return for money or goods, and if you
reserve your lovemaking for the evenings alone, after
he's wined and dined you, it begins to feel very much as
though you're giving him a sexual service in return for
his dollars. Do it when *you* want to, on *your* demand.
He won't think of you as a harlot, but as an independent woman who has her own appetites. He'll realize
that if he wants to keep you happy, he'll have to give as
well as take. The most erotic playmate is the woman
who brings out the best in her lover and herself, and
that's what sex in surprising places and at surprising
times will do.

So he's sitting there one afternoon watching a baseball
game on television? Go in there, if you feel amorous,
and turn him on. So he's working late at the office? Go
around there and don't wear any panties, and see how
long he can concentrate. So he's washing the car? Go out
there in a white blouse with no bra underneath, and see
how long he can go on washing when it turns
transparent with water.

It might seem as if you're being sexually aggressive
and dominant when you do things like that, but don't

worry that your lover will feel diminished by it. He won't. It's still up to him to take you up to bed, or down onto the living room carpet, and produce an erection to make it all work. And when it's all over he'll feel pleased with himself for having chosen such a sexy woman, and self-satisfied that he can make love like a red-hot stud any time of the day or night, any place you care to name. Women often underestimate the size of the male sexual ego. It takes a great deal to make a man believe that *he* wasn't the one who dominated your love-making. An exciting woman exploits that ego to her own—and his—advantage.

If you can't get out of the house to have sex in an un-usual location, look around you. There's the kitchen, the living room, the hallway, the bathroom. Have you made love in all of those rooms yet? Have you made it in the shower? Have you made it on the stairs? What about the back seat of the car while it's in the garage? What about the bushes in your garden at night?

If you want to pump some real life into your loving, take it out of the bedroom and into the fields and the woods and anywhere your imagination can think of. The worst you can get is a sunburn, and the best you can get is terrific.

# 14.

## *Kinky Kapers*

"Some moments in life I could wish very long
  Because as the monkey said, pleasant but wrong
'Tis sweet to remember some frolics I've had
Though the angel who suffered them cries out 'Too
    bad.' "

             —"An Epistle to a Lady," 19th century

When I was editing *Forum*, the sex advice magazine,
a woman wrote to me and said that her husband wanted
her to shave off all her pubic hair. "Do you think," she
asked, "that this is perverted?"

When we start getting into kinky sex, we start getting
deep into a jungle of personal taste and predilection,
and it's very difficult to sort out one man's kick from another man's disgust. *I* don't happen to think it's perverted if a husband wants his wife to remove all her pubic
hair, but I know people who do. Who's right and who's
wrong?

If your lover starts expressing an interest in tying you
up to the bedpost, or dressing up in women's clothing,
or getting you to whip him, or in urination or defaca-
tion, or in rubber or leather, or in making love in a
bathtub full of marshmallows, then I believe there are
two very important things for you to think about.

First of all, do you think your lover wants to do them
because they'll add some spice and excitement to your
sex life, or do you think he wants to do them because
that's the only way he can get his rocks off? If whipping

or bondage or whatever is *essential* for him to achieve satisfactory sex, then you'll have to admit that he is a deviant. If you're going to stay with him, and keep on loving him, his sexual deviation will have to be part of your relationship.

There's nothing to be frightened of in sexual deviation, unless it involves genuinely dangerous practices, in which case you'd be well advised to leave well enough alone. If your lover happens to enjoy wearing high heels and ladies' panties, and you don't mind him wearing them, you could have a perfectly long and happy sex relationship. In fact, if you show you appreciate and understand that they turn him on, he'll be more devoted to you than you could imagine.

But secondly, you have to decide whether you enjoy kinky sex or not. There is no point in going on with any relationship if your lover insists that you do things that you don't like. I think it's important that you should try a few kinks out, in the most unprejudiced way you can, because you might find that something that *sounds* revolting is in fact rather pleasant. But if, after trying it, you find it really leaves you more than cold, you'll have to put your foot down. "Either that wet-suit goes or I do, and that's that."

Remember that a lot of couples who are quite sexually straightforward have found that they can borrow techniques and equipment from some of the major sexual deviations and derive a great deal of fun and pleasure from them. Here's Nina, 32, talking about bondage:

"One night my husband Paul came home with some lengths of cord for his boat. When we went to bed that night, he suddenly came in from the living room holding this cord, and I said: 'What are you going to do with that?' He said: 'I'm going to tie you up.' I just laughed at first, but then he actually caught hold of my wrists and bound them up to the rails at the top of the bed, so tightly that they hurt. I was shrieking at him to let me go, but then he tied each of my ankles to the bottom of the bed, so that my legs were wide apart.

"I shouted at him: 'Let me go! It hurts!' but he wouldn't. He stripped off his clothes and climbed on top of me. He kissed me but I bit his tongue. I was struggling to get free the whole time. Then he went down the bed and started licking my pussy, and there wasn't a damn thing I could do about it. I squirmed about, but suddenly I realized the whole thing was turning me on. I stopped shouting at him because it wasn't doing any good anyway, and he licked me and licked me until I thought I'd go crazy. Then he climbed on top of me again, and his cock was amazing, it was so big, and he pushed it into me and screwed me like that. I had an incredible climax, and somehow it was all the more intense because I couldn't move. When it was over, he untied me, and was really nice to me."

Paul wasn't a real bondage freak. He was just putting an erotic fantasy into practice. As it turned out, he never did it again, and it probably wouldn't have been half as good the second time, because the essence of the fantasy was that Nina was held down against her will. Next time, she would have known what to expect, and would have been much more submissive.

Genuine bondage fetishists go to the most elaborate lengths to tie themselves up, and they get their real kicks from the feeling of masochistic helplessness that results. They buy handcuffs, leg irons, straitjackets, and manacles, and spend more time relishing knots than cunts. They will often visit prostitutes who specialize in bondage and punishment, and pay handsome sums of money to be tied up and humiliated. Monique von Cleef, the Dutchwoman who can probably claim to be the Queen of Pain, tells me that the type of men who come to her for this kind of treatment are often eminent businessmen and civil servants—men who somehow feel guilty for the power they wield in everyday life, and who are looking for someone else to dominate them, rob them of all responsibility, and punish them.

To give you some idea of the lengths to which Miss von Cleef's clients will go, she will often hang them upside down by their heels from the ceiling, trussed up like turkeys, and administer enemas into their upturned anuses. Others like to have 20-pound weights hung by wire from their balls, and some want to sit in playpens and be told baby stories. This might seem like bizarre exaggeration, but I have visited her house in The Hague and actually seen this happen.

While your lover probably doesn't go to these extremes, it's worth remembering that there's a little touch of the masochist in almost every man—along with a streak of sadism, too. If you bite and scratch a man during sex, he will often get an extra thrill out of the pain. Whether you want to go any further into the field of torture and punishment is up to you, but remember that there can be dangers.

Never, ever let a man tie anything around your neck, and never agree to tie anything around his neck. There are people who get a kick out of almost strangulating themselves, but as the police have told me, a lot of them go just a little too far in their search for erotic thrills, and end up in the mortuary.

Make sure you know your lover very well before participating in anything to do with whips or bondage. Even though the man may not actually be homicidal, he may get sexual pleasure from inflicting real pain, and you could end up seriously injured. If it looks as though your date is that kind of man, exit gracefully without panicking and without apparent fear. It will often be your terror that turns him on. What's more, never ever laugh at a violent man. There are too many cases of women who have died for their mockery of a would-be rapist to make the subject at all funny.

After that salutary comment, you might be feeling less like kinky sex. But there are still plenty of things that you and your lover can do that are nonviolent and which can give you both a great splurge of pleasure.

Rubber is one. There is a whole wide (and presumably bouncy) world of rubber fetishists. These are men and women who get a kick out of dressing up in custom-made rubber dresses and suits. They have their own magazines and their own clubs, and they often spend hundreds of dollars on exotic garments and equipment. Many of them overlap into the area of bondage, and some of them enjoy having tight rubber masks laced over their heads, with only a rubber valve to breath through, but these are more extreme types. Milder addicts get sufficient pleasure, believe it or not, from simply dressing up in raincoats and parading up and down in front of each other.

Rubber itself has some peculiarly sensual qualities. It's stretchy, it has a distinctive smell, and it clings. I've asked dozens of rubber fetishists what the exact appeal of it is, but they can never quite define it. You and your lover may be able to find out if you try making love in rubber sheets, or try out some of the cheaper rubber costumes.

Other materials which arouse erotic response in some people are silk, satin, and leather. Satin sheets are available almost anywhere today, and certainly give your bed a sexy new feel to it—something that could be a substitute for seeking erotic pleasure out of doors if it's snowing too hard. You can still buy silk chemises, too, which some men find arousing, and actress Honor Blackman, who played Pussy Galore in *Goldfinger*, first made her name among enthusiastic male TV viewers by walking around in a black leather cat suit.

*Forum* magazine attracted a great many letters from men and women who were aroused by urination (the technical name for this kink is *urolagnia*). Lots of women, when they're making love, feel an urge to pee, and some actually find that they can't stop themselves from releasing a little urine when they reach a climax. This is because many intercourse positions put pressure on your bladder, and the muscular spasms of your orgasm will lead you to spurt a little out. It's quite normal, and nothing to be ashamed of, and your lover won't mind half as much as you think.

Some people, however, go further than that, and actually derive pleasure from watching their partners pass water. If your lover asks you to do that, don't worry about it, he's only getting a kick from seeing you behave like the woman you are. If he wants to be even more outré, though, and asks you to pee all over him, or let him drink your urine, or if he wants to pee all over you, then that's something you'll have to make up your own mind about. If you want to do it, do it; if you don't, refuse.

What if he wants to push things up your vagina or anus?

Again, the same two rules apply. Don't let him shove anything dangerous up you, and only do it if you get some pleasure from it. A porno magazine I saw in Sweden shows two young Chinese girls having peeled bananas pushed into their pussies, and then eaten out by lustful young men. That, to my mind, is a quite acceptable kink which could be fun, although you'd have to have patience. It's hard to be very erotic with a mouthful of banana.

The principal instrument for vaginal insertion is the plastic vibrator, which is roughly penis-shaped. It is safe to insert because it is designed for this very purpose. The vibrator is technology's best contribution for sexual pleasure, and you can use it freely by yourself or in the company of your lover to intensify your sexual sensations without any problems or hangups. Don't let it become essential to your lovemaking, though. *Viva* magazine (the female offshoot of *Penthouse*) once ran a problem-page letter from a woman who found that her vibrator had replaced her husband in her affections, and that she just couldn't get turned on without it.

Two vibrators can be even better than one. A woman I knew used to like pushing a buzzing vibrator up her lover's ass while he did the same to her, and while they both had intercourse. The only warning I'd give about this practice is that neither of you should let go of the end of the vibrator: the muscular contractions of climax could be enough to make the machine disappear up your behind, and the only way to remove it then is by nasty manhandling from a hospital specialist, or possibly even surgery.

The vibrator's superior cousin is the dildo, the artificial penis made of hard latex rubber. You can buy the hand-held version, or the amazing strap-on version, complete with adjustable vibro-motor. They can be a help if your lover has erection trouble, but mostly they're just for fun. Despite what you hear about lesbians using them, incidentally, they are mainly bought by men for use on their mistresses or wives. Lesbians almost always prefer to stimulate each other by cunnilingus or masturbation, eschewing anything so assertively male as a dildo.

A great deal of publicity has been given lately to the ben-wa, or Japanese love balls. Originally ivory, and now inevitably plastic, these are two or more weighted spheres, joined together by a cord, which a woman can insert into her vagina. As she moves, the weights in the balls cause them to shift about and vibrate. They are supposed to stimulate you as you walk about, or rock in a hammock, or do the ironing. The verdict of almost all the women I know who have tried them has been disappointing, though.

The rear-entrance relative of the ben-wa is the Siamese anal necklace. This is a string of tough latex beads which you're supposed to feed into your anus before you make love, and then draw out, bead by bead, when you have a climax. There's no doubt that the necklace does intensify the sensations of orgasm, although some women find them uncomfortable when they're actually having intercourse.

Another gimmick is the love egg, made in Hong Kong, which is exactly what it sounds like: a white plastic egg containing a vibrator. You can rest it on your vulva to stimulate your clitoris, or insert it right inside you. It's on a cord, like a tampon, so it won't get lost.

There's been a recent upsurge, too, in fancy condoms for men. These days they come in all sorts of colors and designs, some of them with ribs and spines and twirly bits on them to give your vagina a little bit more titillation as they slide in and out. If you fancy your man with a purple cock, why not buy him some?

All these "sex-aids" are all right as far as they go, but

like any other gimmick you can rapidly tire of them, whereupon they disappear into your bedside drawer to gather dust. But don't let that put you off using them: even if they give you only a couple of nights of amusement and sexy fun, they're worth it.

When you know your lover better, you can try some kinky underwear on him, too. Almost all women's magazines carry advertisements for exotic nightwear sets and Hollywood undies. Appearing at the bedroom door in a transparent baby-doll top and a pair of split-crotch panties, though, will probably work better on an older man than it will if your lover is younger. To the young, gear like this tends to smack of burlesque shows and bald heads, and the design of most of the items, with feather trimmings and frou-frou nylon, doesn't do much to update the image. Try a tiny pair of plain white panties instead, or a shirt with nothing else on underneath. Alex Comfort, in *The Joy of Sex*, suggests you make your own G-string, but the design he provides won't turn anybody on but the Last of the Mohicans.

Grease and oil can be erotic. Some lovers get a thrill out of smearing each other all over with baby oil, and then making love like a pair of slippery seals. Then there's honey, cream, and other gook: try dipping your lover's cock into a pot of maple syrup and licking it meticulously clean. It's hell on the figure, but I'm sure he'll enjoy it.

Then, like the woman who wrote to me at *Forum*, you could try shaving off all your pubic hair. Many men are very aroused by the sight of bare genital lips, and you don't have to keep them that way forever if you both grow tired of it. The way to remove your pubic hair is to clip it with scissors as close as you can before shaving, then soap the genital area and trim away all the hair with a safety razor. Electric razors have more of a sexy buzz to them, but they don't do the job so well.

Just like a man's beard, your pubic hair will start sprouting as stubble almost every day, so to prevent itching you will need to reshave yourself as often as he does. If your vaginal area starts getting sore, try using a depilatory cream instead. If irritation still persists, call it a day and start growing the bushes again.

If you want to be sexually aggressive, you could insist that your lover shave off all *his* pubic hair as well. The male penis without any hair has rather an attractive sculptural look to it, and looks less like a week-old vulture sitting in a rather scraggy nest.

The main point about kinks is this: don't be afraid to do something or suggest something that you think may turn you on. These days, no man is going to think that you're a scarlet woman because you enjoy doing something a little different. In fact, he'll probably appreciate your idea.

But don't start getting into things that degrade you or begin to take over your sex life. The reason you should try kinky sex, after all, is to add some variety to your erotic relationship, and if you get hung up on one kink alone, then deviation has defeated its own object. It's hard for anyone these days to define degradation, but avoid the kind of sexual activity that makes you consistently feel afterwards that you wish you hadn't done it. You're not stuffy or straight or a prude if there are some sexual activities that you can't feel happy with, once you've tried them with an open mind.

So be kinky, but walk tall. Okay?

# 15.

## *Even Kinkier Kapers*

If you're still fired up by the thought of lashing your lover to the bedrail while you push peeled bananas up your pussy, be warned. There are even hotter excitements to come.

The kinks we have just been talking about are fairly common ways of seeking unusual pleasure, if that's not a contradiction in terms. Most sophisticated lovers know about them, even if they don't actually practice them. They're the kind of kinks that won't usually raise a psychiatrist's eyebrows.

But there are some kinks which are very rare and very unusual, and they're likely to stay that way. Because you and your man, and couples just like you, have invented these kinks for yourselves. They're your own personal custom-made kinks, devised to satisfy your own personal sexual fantasies.

Throughout this book, I've tried to make you feel that you have a *right* to your sexual pleasure. Sometimes you have to *earn* this right, by treating your lover well, and by helping him out with his sexual problems. But it's a right that doesn't have any boundaries at all, and it extends as far into the frontier country of sex as you want it to. Your satisfaction, and the satisfaction of your lover, are your only limits.

That's why, if an erotic fantasy bubbles up in your mind, some strange and kinky little variation that you'd like to try, then as long as your lover is happy with the idea of joining in, you ought to run it up the flagpole and see if his cock salutes it.

To give you some idea of how these fantasies develop, and how exciting they can be when you try them out, I've devoted this chapter to women who have gritted their teeth and managed to tell their lovers what their most private sexual longings are. Yours, of course, may be different from any of these women, but I hope that by the time you've come to the end of this book, you'll be ready to go out there and coax your man into bringing your erotic fantasies to life.

First of all, here's Jill, a 26-year-old movie publicist from New York: "There was one particular sexual fantasy which I'd had for years and years, ever since I was about thirteen or fourteen. I'd never done anything about it, because I was just too embarrassed ever to tell anyone else about it. I couldn't even tell my best friend, let alone a *boy*. I used to think about this fantasy when I masturbated myself, and I sometimes used to think about it when I was making love to men, and in both cases it kind of helped me to come off sometimes, but it really never occurred to me that I could do it for *real*.

"In this fantasy, I guess I'm some kind of slave girl or something. The details vary. Sometimes it's in a kind of Eastern harem, and other times it's in an ordinary city apartment. But I know that I'm a slave, and I have to walk around nude all day, and I'm nothing but the sexual plaything of anyone who comes along. If a man who comes to visit the apartment wants to casually fuck me up against a door, then I have to let him do it. The idea of that really turns me on.

"One of the things I have to do is put on these kind of erotic performances every time visitors come around to see the guy who's in charge of me. Maybe they're having coffee or drinks or talking business. I have to sit there and try to amuse them sexually. I sit on a big leather chair, and I lift my legs up and hook them over the arms of the chair, so that my thighs are wide apart and everyone in the room can see my open cunt.

"I stretch the lips of my cunt wide apart with my fingers, so that the guests can see right up me. Then I push a candle up my cunt, and they can watch it go right in. I masturbate with the candle, thrusting it in and out of me, and moaning and gasping, and clutching my breasts and pinching my own nipples. Then I turn over so that I'm kneeling on the chair, with my upraised bottom facing all the guests, and masturbating even harder with the candle. I invite one of the guests to push another candle up my ass. It hurts when he does it, but everybody just laughs when I cry out with the pain, and the guest takes the candle and rams it straight up my ass until it's more than halfway in.

"I go on and on, masturbating really feverishly, until I have an orgasm, and all the guests sit there, clapping their hands politely, while I'm twisting and turning about with a candle up my cunt and a candle up my ass.

"This fantasy was so kind of—well, *direct*—that I never thought of telling anybody about it. But one night, after I'd been living with Howard for two or three months, we were lying in bed talking about our secret sex desires. It turned out that Howard had always wanted to make blue movies, and we laughed about this, and then he asked me what my secret sex desire was. I didn't want to tell him at first, but bit by bit I plucked up the courage, and I explained it.

"Then he said, 'I have a great idea. Why don't you do your sex fantasy and I'll do mine.' I said 'What do you *mean?*' He said 'You sit there and give me a sex show and I'll make a movie of it.'

"So that's what we did. We chose a special evening when we knew that none of our friends were going to drop by. We had a light supper and a bottle of wine or two. Then Howard set up a movie light, and loaded up his camera, and I took off my clothes and sat on the chair. At first I was shy and awkward. Can you imagine that? I'd been living with the guy for three months and I was shy. But the whole reason was because, really for the first time ever, I was showing him what my sex thoughts were actually like.

"But I knew there was only one way this was going to work, and that was if I acted out the fantasy the way I used to fantasize about it. I had to *believe* I was a slave, and that I was really giving an erotic show. So I let myself relax, and I let myself go, and I did it. I shut my eyes and forgot about Howard and his movie camera. He was getting his rocks off his way, and I was getting my rocks off in my way, and we were both turning each other on. I wriggled my bottom around on that chair, and I stretched my legs wide apart and put my fingers in my cunt and opened it up. Howard came in real close and filmed my cunt from about an inch away. Then I began to work a candle up myself. It felt different from the way I had fantasized about it—it was bigger and harder. But it was still sexy, and I began to have a very strange feeling in my cunt when I watched the candle slide up into me, until there was only about two or three inches showing out of my wide-open lips. It was like having an enormous cold slippery cock up inside me, and I started to work it in and out without even thinking whether this was the way the fantasy went or not.

"I turned over, and I said to Howard, 'The other candle—the other one,' and he took the other candle I had ready, and he greased it up with Vaseline, and he tried to push it up my ass. The feeling was incredible, but the candle was too big and too hard and I couldn't get it up me. It didn't matter, though, when he was trying to force it into me I was so involved with the fantasy that I started to have my orgasm. Howard still has the movie of it. I'm just crouched in that chair, absolutely glistening with sweat, pushing that candle in and out of my cunt as though it's the most desperate thing ever.

"After it was all over, I thought I might be ashamed or something, but I wasn't. I don't see why any woman should be ashamed of a sexual thought she's had, especially when it turns her lover on as well. Yes, I guess it's kinky to push candles up yourself while your lover takes movies of you. Sure, it's kinky. But that's what makes our sex life so exciting. I've done it two or three times since then, and it turns us on more and more every time."

Nobody *taught* Jill how to put on an erotic show like that. It was an idea that came out of her own mind. But so many women are embarrassed to admit they have "dirty thoughts," and fewer still would ever dare to put them into living, loving, practice, the way that Jill did. Yet once she was able to overcome her initial shyness, Jill found that she had discovered a new and exclusive kink that aroused both herself and her lover more than any book-learned variation ever could.

You could do what Jill did with your own private fantasy. All it needs is a little nerve, one or two martinis, and a man to try it on.

This is Petra, 24, a saleswoman from New York, describing how she acted out her own fantasy for her lover, and gave them both a galvanizing experience:

"I don't know how the whole thing started, really. You can never remember how a fantasy starts. It kind of builds up in your mind, and you elaborate on it, and gradually it becomes more and more complicated until finally it doesn't turn you on any more, and you start fantasizing about something else.

"I used to fantasize that I was like Sleeping Beauty, you know. I was dead but I wasn't dead, and I was lying in a tomb, perhaps, or someplace like that. I was aware but I couldn't move. Either I was dead or I'd taken some kind of paralyzing drug. It wasn't really important which it was. The important thing was that I could *feel* things, you see, but I couldn't move or respond to anything.

"So I was lying there in this kind of coma when a man appeared in the tomb. In my fantasy, he was very tall and muscular, and he was only wearing a kind of leather strap around his waist, with a big sword in it, and underneath the strap his penis was just hanging free. He had wild shoulder-length hair, and he was incredibly handsome.

"He saw me lying there on the tomb, and he walked up to me and looked down into my face. I couldn't move, or blink, or do anything to show him that I was alive. He touched my face with his fingers, and then he leaned forward and kissed me. I felt a huge attraction and love for him, but I was completely unable to move a single muscle.

"He ran his hands over my naked body. He touched and fondled my breasts and my nipples. I've always had sensitive breasts, anyway, and the feeling of having them touched and not being able to do anything about it was almost more than I could take. I wanted to move my hips around, and coax him into making love to me, but there was nothing at all I could do.

"He kissed my breasts and nipped my nipples between his teeth. Then his hands went straying down toward my stomach, and around my hips, and soon I could feel his fingers caressing my thighs, and up toward my vagina. The sensation was so strong I would have done any-thing if only I could have moved, but I simply couldn't. I could see him from where I was lying. His backside was rounded and hard, and because he had been stroking me, his penis was erect, and it looked so long and tense, with a beautiful upward curve on the shaft of it, and that incredible shape of the end of it, blunt and mauve-colored and tight.

"After a while, I could feel his fingers fondling my pubic hair, twisting it around his rings. Then he gently touched my clitoris, and it was like nothing on earth, it was so incredible. He rubbed my clitoris until my vagina was wet, and still I could only lie there, dead and cold and still, like a kind of living corpse.

"The man climbed up on top of me, with his penis sticking up and his huge sword hanging down by his side. He held himself up on his muscular arms, and then he lowered himself down gently and smoothly, and the end of his penis parted my vagina like the way you press your thumb into soft fruit, and his shaft ran long and hard right up into my body until I could feel his pubic curls right up against my clitoris.

"He made love to me slowly and teasingly for hours and hours. Sometimes he kept his penis buried inside me and made it twitch and swell with his muscles alone. At other times, he made love, in and out, very fast and even, so that I knew I would have to reach an orgasm sooner or later. But how can a corpse have an orgasm?

"Well, I don't know the answer to that, but I know how I had an orgasm in my fantasy. Instead of centering on my clitoris, like it usually does in real life, it kind of spread inwards from my hands and my feet, soaking toward the center of me like hot liquid soaking into cloth. There seemed to be a kind of red-out, then a black-out, and then it was over. But the pleasure was to-tal. I hadn't moved, but every nerve in my whole body had felt sexual excitement.

"The man climbed off me. His penis was long and limp again, but now it shone with the wet from my va-gina. He thought I was dead, so he didn't even look at me again. He just went striding off to do whatever he had to do next—slaying dragons, I guess.

"I thought about this fantasy over and over again, and every time I thought about it, the more sexy it seemed to be, and the more I invented details to make it sexier still. Then, one evening, I was out with Gil, my boyfriend, for the evening, and the whole fantasy seemed to happen, in real life. It was partly because I wanted to act it out, but also it was partly accidental.

"We had a real stupid argument. It was something to do with his mother. I hate Gil's mother, even though I've tried to like her, and he absolutely dotes on her, so you can imagine that it doesn't make for too good a discussion point. Anyhow, we'd had our usual argument about her, and I was tired, so I went to bed. It was a hot night—August—and I lay on top of the sheets, naked, and closed my eyes and pretended to sleep.

"I must've been there an hour or so. I almost *was* asleep. But then I heard footsteps in the bedroom, and I opened my eyes just a crack and I saw Gil tiptoeing in. He was naked, and the way his penis was hanging there suddenly reminded me of my fantasy. I guess under normal circumstances I would have moved or said something, but somehow I wanted the fantasy to *happen*, so I lay there frozen stiff and still, and I didn't say a word.

"Gil leaned over and kissed my forehead. I still didn't stir. I didn't even open my eyes. Then I felt him kissing my lips, and my neck, and his fingers gently massaging my breasts. When his fingers started to roll my nipples around, and I was getting more and more turned on, I began to wonder whether I'd be able to keep still. But somehow it was more sexy if I did, so I resisted the temptation to move.

"His fingers went over me just like the fingers of the man in the fantasy. They went over my stomach and around my thighs, and then I felt a finger around my clitoris, and a finger slipping up inside my vagina. I quivered a little then, but I kept my eyes shut and I didn't move any more than that. Then another finger went up inside me, and a third finger up my bottom. He began to squeeze and fondle me with these three fingers, and even though my vagina was really wet, I managed to stay cool.

"He climbed on top of me. He kissed my face. I felt his hand opening my vagina, and then the round top of his penis against it. He leaned forward, and it went right up me.

"I knew he was thinking that I'd have to start responding then. But I didn't. I don't know how I managed to stay so still, because it isn't easy when a man's penis is pushing in and out of you, but I did.

"The frustration of not moving seemed to turn me on even more. I felt feelings I've never had before in my life. And it seemed to turn Gil on more as well, because he was building up to a climax much more quickly than I've ever known him to do before.

"I couldn't help moving when I came. Gil said something soft under his breath, and the next thing I knew he was coming. All my control just snapped then, and I think I shrieked out loud. We held on to each other so tight our nails were digging right into each other's skin. When it was finally over, I couldn't speak for ten minutes. The words just wouldn't come.

"We don't play this fantasy very often. Sometimes we do it when we've had an argument. Other times I tease him by pretending to be asleep. We call the fantasy 'playing dead,' but it's not really like making love to dead people or anything sick like that. The whole point is that both of you know that the girl can really feel things, and the fact that she's not allowed to move is what makes it sexy."

I have had letters from men and women who practice almost every variation you can think of, and a few dozen you can't. Some are pretty heavy stuff, and anyone who considers getting into them needs a sound life insurance policy. But a kink needn't be heavy to be outrageous, arousing, and very individual. It's the surprise of the kink, the novelty of it, that will turn your lover on. It will show him something that he has probably never come across in a woman before—a fertile erotic imagination, and a willingness to play it out for real. That will be more than a bonus mark in making you the kind of woman that he won't be able to forget.

Try this personalized kink of Yvonne, a 28-year-old singer from Duluth:

"I didn't even think that what I liked was kinky until some boyfriend of mine said, 'Boy, you sure are kinky.' Kinky is only comparative, if you know what I mean. If everybody was kinky, then nobody would be kinky. It's only because most people are so goddam *straight*.

"I'm crazy about having sex in fast cars. It's almost like a drug. I've never had any fantasies about it—not before I first did it, anyway, but after I'd done it once, I found it gave me such a kick that I wanted to do it again and again.

"Sure, it's scary, but that's what makes it such a thrill. I can still remember the first time I did it. I was out with a man called Andy, and he'd taken me for cocktails and I was flying pretty high. In fact, I think we both were. He drove an English sports car, I think it was an E-Type Jaguar. Tiny, you know, but so *fast*. After the party he was driving me home, and you have to realize that up until then, we had never done anything intimate, no sex.

"He asked me if I liked to drive fast, and I said *sure*. And Jesus, did he drive fast. We went down that highway like there was all the demons out of hell on our tail. I sat there kind of exhilarated and terrified both at the same time. It actually made me feel sexually excited. Can you imagine that? I was so afraid that I was turned on. I clung on to Andy's arm, and dug my nails in, and I looked at the speedometer and he was doing about a hundred and ten. It was night, you know, and there was thick traffic, and he was . . . well he was crazy.

"I reached over while he was driving and I put my hand right on the front of his pants. I gripped his cock through the fabric, and I rubbed it around and around, and I felt it grow hard and big in my hand. If there was any way, I would have fucked him then and there. He just gave this big sigh of satisfaction when I held him there, and he practically burst out of his pants.

"We were still doing more than a hundred when I managed to struggle his zipper open and take out his bare cock. The tires were screaming on every curve, and the engine was roaring like a beast. There was a beautiful smell of cock when I took him out, and there was that fantastic fat purple head, and it was already all juicy and slick. I lifted my dress up and tugged down my own panties, just to show him how much I wanted him, and then I bent forward into his lap and I started to give him head, and I masturbated myself at the same time.

"Down there, with his gorgeous fat cock filling my mouth up, I couldn't even see what was happening on the road. I could feel the car bouncing and I could hear the engine and the wind, but it was weird and frightening, and I wondered if we'd crash and die at the same time as having a climax. I sucked at him and felt scared to death, and just when I felt I had to look, his come just jumped up into my mouth. I didn't have an orgasm myself, not that time, but almost every time I have sex in a fast car now, I managed to reach the top. Once I even fucked a boyfriend when he was driving. I sat on his lap and he looked around me. I think if anyone had caught us we would have been thrown into jail."

It's hard to associate with other women's personal kinks, I know. They are, after all, a matter of taste. But it's important to know that you *can* act out your most secret sexual whims if you have enough courage, enough passion, and the kind of man you want to act them out with.

As a woman, your sexual identity has been suppressed for far too long—by rigid sexual morality and by male domination. If you have erotic whims and desires of your own—no matter how fantastic and kinky they may be—it is worth trying to express them. You will quickly learn which fantasies can become part of your love life and which fantasies are best left as daydreams. Your sex relationships will be enriched with erotic variations from your own imagination, and you will be *developing* as a sexual human being.

What's more, you will stimulate and arouse the man you love, giving him the kind of sex life that probably only existed for him before in *his* fantasies.

# 16.

## *Eat, Drink, and Be Sexy*

"If music be the food of love, play on . . ."
—Shakespeare

There are still plenty of people around who believe in aphrodisiacs—potions or powders or foods that can actually turn you on. You can still read stories of lecherous men "slipping something" into a woman's drink, after which the unfortunate lady, prim though she normaly is, turns into a raving nymphomaniac.

Victorian gentlemen used to drink rather a lot of cocoa to inflame their desires, and there is a hilarious orgy sequence in one English underground magazine of the late nineteenth century which describes how a whole crowd of girls were fired into a state of unquenchable lust on hot chocolate alone.

Almost every food has at one time or another been ascribed erotic power. The Romans used to cover their fruit and desserts with silver and gold, in the belief that precious metals improved the sexuality, and you can still buy tablets today that are silver-covered, and which are alleged to do wonders for your libido.

Fennel, oranges, rose petals, *pâté de foie gras*, oysters, eggs, ginger, and sea holly were all supposed to be aphrodisiacs. And right up until the eighteenth century, eager lovers were compounding and taking love philters made up of mandrake and bat's blood and all other kinds of creepy glop.

But the sad truth is that no food or drug known to man can have the physical or mental effect of arousing sexuality. Even Spanish Fly, or cantharides, the most renowned of aphrodisiacs, is a flop. In fact, it's a dangerous flop, because it irritates the genitourinary tract, and can kill you.

If a lover of yours ever produces any kind of chemical and claims that it's an aphrodisiac, (1) don't try it, because it could be lethal, and (2) think to yourself whether a man who believes he needs chemicals to turn you on is sexy enough for you anyway.

Some drinks, foods and drugs can put you into the mood for love, but they do this by invigorating you or relaxing you. Alcohol, taken strictly in moderation, peels away your inhibitions, and under its influence you will find that you're prepared to be sexier and dirtier than you normally would be. Don't, however, give too much alcohol to your lover, because it has the dual effect of relaxing both his inhibitions and his cock.

Marihuana is commonly supposed to be an aid to sexuality, but there is little evidence for this. It has the effect of heightening any mood you happen to be in, and if you're already in a sexy mood, it can make intercourse more colorful, but it also has a decidedly drooping effect on men.

As far as food is concerned, light and spicy meals can help you feel sexually turned on, but digestion is usually the enemy of copulation. Many women make the mistake of assuming that a rich and substantial meal will arouse their lover's passions, but it's far more likely to send him to sleep. History and psychology tell us that there were, and still are, many people for whom food is a *substitute* for sexual activity, rather than an adjunct, because it dulls the libido.

The way you eat, however, can improve your sex life. If you eat smallish meals regularly, your digestive tract will never be so gorged that you find lovemaking uncomfortable. And if you eat to stay slim, you will not only look better in your lover's eyes, you will be healthier and fitter and much more ready for the frolics of bedtime.

Always start the day by eating something—preferably a couple of eggs and some fruit juice and toast. By the time midday comes around, you'll feel less like filling up on fattening sandwiches, hamburgers, cakes, or cookies. At lunch, eat something light like fish or meat with a salad. Drink wine rather than beer or spirits, because it's less fattening. Don't, of course, take sugar and cream in your coffee.

In the evening, eat something with plenty of protein in it, like a steak or a pork chop, with fresh vegetables. Avoid sauces, and broil or roast your food rather than fry it. Go easy on potatoes, rice, and other cereals. Bread and ice cream are the lover's worst enemies.

When you're cooking for your lover, don't prepare anything so elaborate that you have to spend half the evening in the kitchen. I was treated to a beautiful Chinese meal once, but I only caught occasional glimpses of my girlfriend as she rushed in to gobble a few noodles before dashing back into the kitchen to decorate yet another dish. Chinese food is okay, but it comes in lots of small bowls, which means endless dishwashing as well.

Try something simple, but make it distinctive by adding an unusual sauce or side dish—something that will make him *remember* the meal. Most men find it hard to recollect what they had for breakfast, let alone what they had for dinner two weeks ago, and so something that's out of the ordinary will help you and your cooking stay in his mind.

You could have a go at a traditional English erotic salad, which contains several "aphrodisiac" ingredients. Even though it won't actually cause a mighty erection, you can always tell him that it's supposed to turn people on, and the power of mental suggestion could well be enough to do the trick.

You will need:

10 fennel leaves
2 teaspoonfuls of chopped parsley
½ cucumber
10 violet flowers
3 teaspoonfuls sugar

Cut up the cucumber into small pieces, sprinkle the sugar over the violets, and then turn the whole salad in a wooden bowl with French dressing (mustard, olive oil, lemon, and vinegar).

You can serve this salad with almost any kind of meat.

On amorous evenings, I need hardly tell you that it's advisable to avoid very strong spices, particularly garlic. The evening may be amorous, but you don't want to wake up in the morning with your breath smelling unbearable.

Avoid the economic temptation to serve your lover a cheap wine. Since you will shortly be bouncing around in bed, you will find that cheap wine doesn't sit well on the stomach, and there are few feelings less romantic than retching.

The bedtime feast is quite a sexy idea. Instead of bothering with a formal meal, take some crisp-roasted chicken legs, salad, and fruit into the bedroom, and gnaw them naked to the accompaniment of a bottle of chilled dry white wine. Don't forget paper tissues or a couple of damp hand towels, though. You don't want hands glistening with chicken fat running their passionate way through your fresh-washed hair.

In all, be cautious how you mix sex and food. And be even more cautious how you mix sex and drink. If you feel you're over the limit when you're out with a man, stick to tonic water or dry ginger ale. They look as though they're potently alcoholic, but they'll keep you on the right side of an inebriated indiscretion. Although plenty of men try to seduce girls by tanking them up, very few men actually enjoy the spectacle of a drunken woman. You will gain much more respect from your lover if you restrict yourself to a cheerful merriness, and leave the glassy eyes and the slurred speech to the bar-flies.

If, despite all this, you're feeling woozy and out of control, and you're worried that you might do something you're going to regret the next morning, go into the kitchen and mix yourself a couple of raw eggs with Worcestershire sauce and cayenne pepper, and down the lot. That should bring you back to reality in fairly rapid order.

Many hard-drinking men who are planning to go out on a bender quaff a pint of milk beforehand. If you can't manage to do that, at least eat something before you start drinking. Poured into an empty stomach, alcohol is very quickly absorbed into the bloodstream, and you'll be dancing on the tables before you know what's hit you.

Skol, and *bon appétit.*

# 17.

## *Double Your Pleasure, Double Your Fun*

"I knew that Bill used to see a lot of his secretary. They had something special going between them. One day I asked him point-blank if he ever took her to bed, and he said sure, they used to make love maybe once or twice a week. He was totally cool about it, and he said that I ought to know that one woman just wasn't enough for a man—not even if that woman was me.

"Well, I'm not married to Bill, and I don't have any particular dependence on him, except that I love him. But I got to thinking—if he could have two affairs at once, why couldn't I? I asked myself a question I should have asked myself years ago. Maybe one woman wasn't enough for one man—but was one man enough for one woman?

"In Bill's case, one man *wasn't* enough. He was beautiful in bed, but that was about as far as it went. We didn't have very much else in common. He had no eye for culture, didn't understand art. He didn't know Matisse from a mattress, and in any case he would have preferred the mattress. So, in the end, I decided to find me another man, a man who filled a different kind of role in my life, and start a second-string affair.

"All I can say is that the day I decided to do that was the most liberating day of my entire life."

Well—why *not* have two affairs at once?

There might be a couple of convincing arguments against it. You might be completely satisfied with the physical and intellectual capacities of the man you already have. He might be very jealous, and make life so awkward and uncomfortable for you that having two affairs would be more effort than entertainment.

You might not be the type of woman who can do it with a light heart and a clear conscience, and in that event I must simply bow to your principles. Multiple affairs are not easy to handle, and I would rather you stayed happy than tried to reach for something you couldn't cope with.

But, on the whole, women who feel able to venture into the unpredictable but exciting field of double affairs find that the advantages outweigh the snags. They have the unique experience of being able to compare one man's sexual performance with another's—sometimes on the same day—and being able to apply the lessons they have learned from one lover to the affair they are having with the other lover.

"I have only once had an exclusive affair with one guy," said 27-year-old Bernice, from New York. "It was a disaster. I became far too dependent on him—much more dependent than I wanted to be, or he wanted me to be. I know the time will come when I'll be able to settle down with one guy. I don't think he'll be a superman or anything like that. As long as he gives me reasonable satisfaction in bed, and reasonable satisfaction out of bed, then that will be more than anyone could ask for.

"But at the moment, one man just isn't enough for me. I have to lead two lives. I can escape from one life to the other, and they're both different. The two guys I'm going out with at the moment are complete opposites. One is an actor, called Jason, he's very good-looking, with blond curly hair and a beautiful body. But he's very *mannered*, you know. He's not at all gay, but he acts precious. Everything is *fabulous* or *wonderful*, or else it's absolutely *dreadful*. He's great fun to be with, and he's kind and witty, and he makes love well, but that isn't enough by itself.

"My other boyfriend is Ed. He's an engineer, he designs something to do with hydraulics. He's quiet and he's slow and he's strong. He doesn't ask questions and he doesn't tell lies. I can turn up at his apartment almost any time of the day or night, and he hardly says a single word but takes me into his bed, and fucks me slow and at nothing but his own speed. Ed's the kind of guy you can sit with for hours with only a sentence or two between you, and yet you can end the day really satisfied.

"But Ed isn't enough for me on his own. He has none of that bubbling sense of humor that Jason has, and after a few hours I find him too quiet and masculine and withdrawn, so I go back to Jason in search of some fun.

"I'm not sure whether they know about each other. Ed knows that he isn't the only one, and I suspect that I'm not the only one for him.

"But that's not the important thing. The important thing is that, until someone better comes along, Jason and Ed together are just what it takes to satisfy me. I may not be faithful to either one of them, but I'm faithful to both of them, if you see what I mean. I've been dating Jason for four months and Ed for almost a year, and I don't see that there's anything promiscuous about either of those relationships."

If you're the kind of woman who can come to terms

with the idea that you are just as entitled to seek your pleasures wherever and whenever you want to—just as much as a man—you could find that running your affairs two-in-hand gives you a fascinating insight into the sexual behavior of men. You'll be able to compare X's rhythm with Y's, X's loveplay with Y's, and X's whole orgasmic technique with Y's. In other words, you'll be able to see more clearly where X is being clumsy and Y is being smooth, where X is taking more interest in his pleasure than yours, and where Y is tickling your clitoris at just the right moment.

Even more important, though, is the way in which a double-stacked affair situation helps *you*. Provided you're emotionally cool enough to deal with the inevitable extra stresses and strains that *two* ardent lovers can place upon your feminine psyche, you can reap several big benefits.

First—and you must never underestimate the importance of this—is that having two lovers wil give you tremendous confidence in your own sexual atractiveness. Not only does one terrific man want you as his bed partner, but two men do. Two men crave your cunt, your breasts, your kisses, and your company.

"I used to look at myself naked in the mirror," said 20-year-old Jackie, "and I used to feel so goddam proud of myself. I even used to fantasize sometimes that I could have as many lovers as I wanted—not just two, but five or six or a dozen."

Confidence in your sexual attractiveness will greatly help in improving your sexual style. If you know that men are really attracted to you, you must also know that they're being *turned on* by your attractiveness, and you'll worry less anxiously about whether you're exciting them or not. So many women hold back their loveplay and remain stiff and awkward in bed, simply because they're lacking in faith in their own sex appeal. Well, you might doubt your sex appeal when you're dating one man, but there can't be much question that you've got what it takes if you're dating *two*.

A double affair will also help you to gain sexual proficiency more quickly. Everyone learns something about technique from every affair they're involved in, even if they hardly realize it. When you make love to a man, you learn from him (if you're aware and willing to learn) almost everything that he knows about sex, and he's learned that from all the women he's ever slept with.

Even if you stick to one affair at a time, you'll learn quite a lot from plain old experience. But if you have two at a time, or more, you'll have the chance to test and compare what you learn from *one* of your lovers on the *other*.

This is Amy, a 25-year-old fashion buyer, talking about her own two lovers: "When I was younger, I was very naïve about sex. My mother never told me much about it, and although I had a kind of sketchy idea where babies came from, I didn't know anything about having intercourse with a man. I learned a few things from school and college, just from talking to other girls, but of course I didn't really understand.

"I lost my virginity when I was just 19, on my nineteenth birthday, to a man eight years older than me. I found out later he was married. We had a big party at a club I used to go to a lot, and I guess we all had too much to drink. This guy was very charming and he seemed much older and more sophisticated than everybody else there, but when I think now that he was only twenty-seven, he couldn't have been that great.

"He offered to drive me home, and I said yes. I was pretty unsteady on my feet, and I really wasn't sure what was going on. He took me across the parking lot and into the woods, and then he pressed me up against a tree and started kissing me. I didn't resist. I liked him, and I felt stirred up and sexy toward him, so there was no reason why I should.

"He lifted up my dress. I struggled a bit and tried to stop him, but we were both laughing too much. He managed to pull my panties down to my knees, and then to my ankles, and he pushed his hand up between my legs, and started fingering me. I knew my pussy was wet, and that embarrassed me. I think I struggled more because I didn't want him to know how juicy I was, rather than because he wanted to have sex with me. But then he got his fingers up there, and started rubbing my clitoris, and he seemed to like doing it so much that I started to relax a little.

"I couldn't see much in the dark, but I felt his cock pressing up between my legs. He put his finger up me to help him push it into the right place. I knew what was happening, but at the same time I didn't know the right way to react. Before I knew what was going on, he had his cock right up me, and he was thrusting in and out of me, and I remember looking through the darkness at the trees and the car lights in the distance, and thinking to myself, I'm actually having intercourse. I'm actually having it.

"Anyhow, that's how naïve I was. That was the first and only time I had sex with that guy, but later on I met John, and I guess you could say that he became my first serious lover. He wasn't Casanova, but he was sweet and kind, and we had a good thing going for almost a year. Then I dated around a while, and then I met Paul, and when that broke up I met Mac.

"Mac's a wonderful friend and he's also good in bed. He's a script writer for movies. Nothing big, like *The Sting*. But those movies they use to train people, and to stop accidents in factories, that kind of stuff. I met him at a party, and he asked me out to dinner, and the next weekend he took me up to his parents' house in New Hampshire. We walked, read books, and made love over and over again. Mac's gentle and he's educated. He knows all kinds of obscure things, but just because he's gentle that doesn't mean he's weak. He's always so considerate when we make love, he always cares about what I feel, and whether I have a climax or not.

"It's funny, but you don't always want consideration. One night, when Mac was working, I was invited around to meet some friends for drinks. There was a new guy there, a guy I'd never seen before, and someone introduced him to me. His name was Frank. He's quite different from Mac. Frank is one of those men who can always rile you up, no matter if you know he's going to try and do it or not. He had me all steamed up in about five minutes, talking about women in politics, and I'm not even strongly into women's liberation at all. He was also very sexy, although I hardly realized it at first. He wore rough faded denims, and a silver cross around his neck so big you could have used it to keep off Dracula.

"He offered to take me out for a meal—or, rather, he demanded that I come along. Mac was working that night until late, so I didn't see any harm in it. Frank drove me out to a restaurant on the highway somewhere, and we had steaks and salad—nothing fancy, but it was all good stuff.

"He didn't even ask me if I wanted to go back to his place. He had the whole top floor of a big house in the suburbs. It was untidy, like him, and there was more beer in the icebox than food, but it was exactly the kind of place I would have imagined him to live in.

"We had drinks, and he played some music, and then he upped and took me by the hand, and said, 'Let's fuck.' I was flattered and scared, both at the same time. He didn't even try to undress me. He just peeled off his shirt, and took off his jeans, and there he was, standing there naked with his big muscly hairy body, and a massive cock standing up so hard it was practically steaming.

"I didn't say no. I sometimes wonder why I didn't, but I didn't. Frank's not the kind of guy you ever say no to, except in an argument. I took off my slacks, and my panties, and then my blouse and my bra. I stood there in front of him with my hands over my pussy. I felt shy and turned on at the same time. I felt like a lamb all ready for the slaughter. Mac had never made me feel like that.

"We fucked on the floor. It was fucking. Frank was hard and violent and he has an appetite for sex like some people have for pretzels—he never knows when to stop. He fucked me so hard it hurt. I wanted to cry out, but somehow the hurt was too nice to complain about.

"We came once, both together, and the whole thing shook me. Then, after we'd shared a cigarette, he wanted to fuck some more. He told me to come and sit on his face. At first I wouldn't do it. I was full up with his come, and I was sure he didn't want me to . . . well, he did. So he lay back on the floor, and I gingerly squatted myself down over his face. He started kissing and licking my pussy at first. The sensation was fantastic. I could feel his come sliding out of me and on to his lips and down his chin. Then I felt his tongue thrusting at my asshole, and then he actually bit my asshole with his teeth. It hurt, but my God.

"My pussy was so sore after Frank had finished with me. He bit my asshole and my lips and he nipped at my clitoris, and it was painful but it was just incredible. Frank taught me that pain could be erotic as well. I lay there on the floor after we'd finished, and I felt used-up and a bit whoreish, but somehow I was pleased as well.

"Anyhow, the point is that I went back to Mac that same night, and I tried out what I'd learned on him. I knew he wasn't vicious enough to bite me first, so I wriggled my way underneath him, and I licked his asshole, and I bit his balls, and I hurt him so much that he almost screamed. But I was just biting that bit in between his balls and his asshole when he came, all over my breasts, and he came harder and with much more come than I'd ever seen before.

"Over the months, I've been able to teach Frank some of Mac's gentleness, and I've been able to teach Mac some of Frank's cruelty. Right now, I think I have the best sex life I could think of, apart from two of the most fantastic men I can imagine."

I've quoted Amy at length because her personal experience with two men sums up the sexual benefit of having simultaneous affairs better than any advice from me could ever do. But I do have some advice for you on the subject, and it's pretty important. It concerns the whole etiquette of running parallel lovers, and what you should do if your duplicity is discovered.

It's to your own advantage if you can pick for your

delightful duo a pair of men who are fundamentally *opposite* to each other in character and style. This won't always be possible, of course, because you never know whose lust-filled eyes are going to meet yours across that crowded room. But if you can choose one for his brawn and the other for his brains, or one for his sadism and the other for his masochism, or one for his love of animals and the other for his prowess with a Smith & Wesson, then you should have a pretty complementary pair. One of the oddest pair of lovers I know (and this is for real) is the pair who, unbeknownst to each other, are regularly servicing a lady stenographer. One of them is a 48-year-old doctor of philosophy, and the other is a 19-year-old McDonald's hamburger chef.

There is one firm rule which you must always remember when you're involved in double affairs. You must *never* lie. I know this is a difficult rule to keep, but it is essential if you're going to keep your head, your integrity, and if the worst comes to the very worst, and the truth comes out, at least *one* of your two bedmates.

If you lie, your lies will probably find you out. Lovers, or their friends or relatives, have an uncanny knack of walking around corners just as you're involved in soul-kissing your No. 2 man. Or maybe they know someone who saw you driving in a red Corvette along Rockaway Boulevard when you were supposed to be visiting your sick grandmother in New Jersey.

It's better for a man to think that you're allowing someone else to jump on your bones than it is for him to think that you're lying. He can then direct his rivalry, jealousy and enmity against the other man, for seducing you, rather than at *you*, for deceiving him.

If one of your two lovers wants to know why you can't see him, then tell him simply that you're going out with friends. Explain that you're a grown-up lady, and that you have your own life to lead, despite the fact that you love him very much, and wouldn't it be nice if he took down his pants right now and let you give him a nice little feel right between the legs?

A feel tends to cure the most inquisitive of male minds.

Which of your lovers should take priority? Are there times when you should snub one in favor of the other?

If you are simply dating both of them on a temporary basis (in other words, if you haven't much intention of marrying either of them, or living with either of them for the rest of your natural-born days), then it will do *them* good and *you* good if you treat them with Solomon-like equality. Share your time between them reasonably equally, except for special occasions (birthdays, bar mitzvahs, funerals).

Some women with two lovers are fastidious about douching away the evidence of one before meeting the other, but in my view this is a hygiene point that is entirely up to your personal preference. Sperm is not harmful or infectious, except when a man has a venereal disease, and quite a few girls say that one of the pleasures of double-dating is to make love to one man while the semen of the other is still inside them.

"The thought of having two different kinds of sperm, all mixed up inside my vagina at once, is absolutely fantastic," testifies one young secretary.

Just be careful that you don't have so much semen inside you that it is leaking from your vagina before you even *start* making love to your second choice of the day.

Since I've mentioned venereal disease, *do* take reasonable precautions if you suspect that either of your lovers is suffering from gonorrhea or something similar. Watch out for unusual discharges, itching or sores, or painful urination. You might not be your other lover's only love, and if you pass it on to him, he could be passing it on to others, and that's the way venereal disease spreads.

If VD does rear its ugly head, you will have to pluck up courage and admit to your men that they're not the only ones in your life. They're going to find out anyway if they catch the disease, and they'll think much more of you if you make a clean breast of it than if you try to keep it a state secret.

Life will definitely be easier if you keep a diary with basic facts about each of your lovers in it. *Don't*, of course, allow this incriminating document to fall into either of their jealous hands. But it will help you to check quickly on pertinent facts that you might otherwise confuse. It will stop you getting their birthdays mixed up. It will help you remember which one of them took you to see *Towering Inferno* and which one took you to the rock concert.

What should you do, though, if the ultimate exposure happens? If one of them catches you *in flagrante delicto* with the other, at a party, at the theater, or even, heavens preserve you, in bed?

You'll be surprised to learn that you have a fairly good chance of getting away with it all, scot-free. In fact, there is even a chance that you will be able to continue your double-affair relationships just as before, although the chance, I warn you, is slender to paper-thin.

Absolute Rule One: Burst into tears. Not in an ugly or violent way, but just get them big Bambi-like drops of distilled sadness rolling down your cheeks.

This has the effect of arousing the protective instincts in both men. Instead of blaming you, their feelings will be directed toward blaming each other. But there won't be *too* much enmity between them, because they will both feel sympathy for a common cause—you, and your tearful plight.

Absolute Rule Two: Don't argue with either one of them. If you're in public, or at a party, this will only stir up an ugly scene. If you're in private, or in bed, or some other intimate situation, it could provoke violence and make all of you say things that you afterward regret.

Absolute Rule Three: Leave both of them as soon as possible, and go home. If they want to beat each other insensible, then leave it to them. But at least neither one of them will feel that you've left with the other, and be consumed with jealousy.

The following day, call each one of them and explain the situation. Tell them the truth—that you are fond of both of them, and that you found it impossible to make a choice. One or both of them will tell you that you have to make that choice now, even if you couldn't make it before. You can make a choice, if you want to, according to whichever lover you prefer, or you can decide never to see either of them again, or you can mutter and mumble something about love and passion, and continue seeing both of them, still in secret, and carry on as before. It will be up to you to judge how much strain the situation can take.

Some women, of course, always land successfully on their feet (or on their backs). A German girl I knew who was having two affairs at once, and was found out, promptly invited both lovers to bed at the same time, and began a satisfying and long-lasting trio.

Whatever the market will stand, as salesmen are wont to say.

# 18.

## *Orgies and Other Gatherings*

> "There were three in the bed
> And the little ones said:
> 'Roll over! Roll over!' "
> —Nursery song, traditional

Could you stand the thought of sharing your lover with another woman—all in the same bed at the same time?

Or how about the idea of you and your lover and another man?

Threesomes, swinging, swapping and orgies have become very fashionable sexual topics, but they're by no means as simple and uncomplicated as just jumping into bed with a crowd of other people. If you're aiming to be the perfect playmate, it's important for you to sort out in your mind what you think about them, and whether you're the kind of girl who would be willing to give group sex a whirl.

Threesomes, or *troilism* as they're more technically known, tend on the whole to be unplanned events, although some notable men of history have lived for some time with more than one woman at once (Augustus John, the artist, and Charles Mingus, the jazz musician). Also they usually happen between people who are related or know each other extremely well.

This is Moira, a 25-year-old secretary, who shared her lover's bed with her sister Alexandra, and found it wasn't as traumatic an experience as she'd feared:

"Peter had always liked us both, and when I was away last year he dated Alex a couple of times, although purely platonically. Alex was always quieter than me, and never had so many boyfriends, so she often used to come with us to the movies or out for a picnic or something.

"Then about two months ago we decided to hold a party in our apartment. It was very successful, and a lot of people turned up. Alex met a nice guy called Fred, and was dancing with him most of the evening, but when it was all over, I found her sitting by herself in the bathroom in floods of tears. They'd had an argument over something, and Fred had called her a bitch, and it was all pretty unpleasant. Anyway, she cheered up a bit, and we tidied the place up, and then Peter and I went to bed, and Alex was going to sleep on the couch.

"But about halfway through the night, Alex came into the bedroom and got into bed next to me, and was still very upset. I cuddled her, and we went to sleep. The next thing I knew, Peter was moaning in his sleep. I opened my eyes, and Alex was snuggled up next to him, gently rubbing his cock. I felt shocked at first, but then I thought—well, she's my sister, I know her well enough. So I whispered to her, 'Let's wake him up and give him a surprise.'

"So I called in his ear, and he woke up. He looked at me, and he looked at Alex, and he felt the hand on his cock, and didn't know whose it was, and he just said quietly, 'Oh, boy.' The situation turned all three of us on. I started kissing Peter and Alex went down on him and sucked his cock. Then I climbed on top of him, and Alex pushed his cock inside me, and I could feel it all wet with her saliva.

"I was going up and down on Peter's cock while Alex kissed him and fondled his bottom and his balls, and then we changed places, and Alex sat on him. I was holding his balls and I could feel them shudder, and he had his climax. Alex had one, too. Afterwards, Peter stroked me until I came off as well, and then the three of us just put our arms round each other and went to sleep.

"In the morning, Alex was gone. I think that was the best way. I don't know how we would have felt about it in the cold light of dawn."

If your lover suggests sharing your bed with another woman, think about two things very carefully. First—could you take it? Would you be too jealous when it actually came down to watching him have sex with another woman in front of your eyes? Would you be able not only to watch it but participate as well?

Secondly—why does he want to do it? Is it because he's bored with you? Is it because you're bored with him? Is he just trying to put flesh into a secret fantasy of his, or does he genuinely feel that your relationship could be improved and livened up by asking another woman to join in the fun?

Many troilistic experiences start because the women involved are fascinated to find out what a lesbian relationship could be like. Women are often (and quite normally) attracted to other women's bodies. Several women have said to me that they would like to squeeze or fondle another woman's breasts just to see what it feels like. This is the experience of 19-year-old Amelia, an art student:

"One day I was supposed to see Paul in the evening and he phoned just beforehand and said he had a cold and couldn't see me. So I felt very disappointed, and then I thought 'Well, I'll take him some grapes and stuff to cheer him up.' So I bought a whole picnic of lovely cold food and books and—oh, it makes me bitter when I remember. Anyway of course I rang the bell and he came to the door in just his trousers and he looked rather annoyed at first, and then he smiled in a rather sinister way and said, 'Ah, Amelia, just what we wanted some company.' And then he led me through to the bedroom and—there was another girl. All undressed and she had a horrible plastic dildo-thing in her hand. And I sort of choked and rushed back, but Paul caught me and kissed me and was very gentle and said, 'No, don't mind her, come back,' And then he said, 'Anne, this is your new playmate,' and this horrible dykey girl came and put her arms around me as well, while Paul sort of held me so I couldn't go. And they both pulled my clothes off and she kept jamming her huge breasts in my face and it was really foul. And then Paul held my arms up behind my back so it really hurt while this really tough girl—I'm sure she was a lesbian—felt all down my front and ... and, you know, with her fingers ... put her fingers inside me. And I can't quite remember what happened then but the next thing I knew I was on the bed—I think Paul had been making love to me and I thought she'd gone away, but then she reappeared and ... Well if you must know she sort of sat down over my face, I mean she was naked and everything and it was all wet, and then Paul was screwing me and saying in this soft voice, 'You must suck her, Amelia. Go on. Go on, be nice to Anne.' And you know it was very peculiar because—I was enjoying him screwing me and I sort of almost wanted to do what he said, you know, to this girl, and actually I couldn't help it because I was so powerless. I don't think I'm a lesbian. I can't be a lesbian, can I? It wasn't my fault, I mean it was sort of rape, but if

I'm honest with myself, I have to admit the really awful thing—that I did like it, the woman and everything. I mean I actually enjoyed it."

Amelia's feelings were not unusual. All of us—both women and men—have slight homosexual tendencies. We appreciate erotic appeal in our own sex. And there is nothing weird or peculiar in wanting to make love to someone of our own sex if and when the opportunity presents itself. We might feel ashamed of ourselves afterwards, but just because you've kissed another woman, that doesn't mean to say you've automatically turned into a lesbian. Lesbianism isn't *catching*, like the flu.

Paul's behavior in this situation was not very understanding or pleasant, and he was obviously indulging a selfish erotic fantasy with no thought of either woman's feelings. If your lover really wants you to join in with him and another woman, I just hope that he approaches you with more tact and sympathy. Otherwise, tell him it's time he was moseying along.

Troilistic sessions with two women and one man, although they're an ideal male chauvinist daydream, are not usually as sexually satisfactory as threesomes with two men and one girl. Since few men can manage more than one shot per half-hour, two women relationships usually end up with the women making love to each other while the man, drooping and disappointed, watches them enjoy themselves and hopes for normal service to resume as soon as possible.

When there is just one woman (you), one man can rest and restore his energy while the other makes love to you.

The main kick that men get out of two-man threesomes is in watching another fellow making love to their woman, which appeals to the male predilection for *visual* excitement. It's up to you to decide whether you feel like being used by your lover as a kind of erotic peep-show.

The appeal and success of a threesome depends entirely on the natures and personalities of the people involved. If it's not your cup of tea, don't be all uptight and shocked if your lover suggests it. It doesn't mean he's bored with you or that he's a mad kinky sex-fiend. It simply means that he sees your relationship in a slightly different sexual light from you, and that to him, having intercourse is not an exclusive and private practice. You can always say, "No," after all.

If you do decide to give troilism a try, remember that there are some firm and sensible rules attached to it. If you're joining an existing couple, married or going steady, as the stranger at the feast, you may find that suddenly you're the center of a domestic blitz of jealousy, either from the wife or from the husband. In the event of this happening, don't join in the fight. If it goes on growing worse, then simply get dressed, say good-night, and leave them to get on with it.

If you yourself are one of the "host couple," then have the sense to be *quite sure* before you start leaping around with another man or woman that you're not going to suddenly feel jealous and sore. If your emotions do boil over, then explain quietly and calmly how you feel about it, and quit on the spot. Don't let yourself be coaxed back into the session, because that'll only make it worse.

Never take sides in a troilistic session, and don't gossip about one partner behind the other's back. Not only is it bad manners, but you could abruptly find that you've misjudged the feelings of the other two, and you're suddenly the odd one out.

What about swinging and swapping, key parties and all that stuff?

Well, I might sound very straight and starchy about it, but I have seen and talked to enough people involved in activities like these to recommend you to stay as clear as you possibly can. They are, almost without exception, emotional disaster areas.

I'm not putting down the spontaneous orgy which happens at an up-tempo party between friends, lovers, and whoever happens to have walked in. What I'm against are the deadly organized sex parties that a certain type of middle-class suburbanite uses in the vain pursuit of sexual excitement. Although many people claim that wife-swapping is one way to inject new life into a dog-eared marriage, it appears to me that it is the final admission of no-hope. It is a way of committing adultery with the knowledge and consent of one's marriage partner, and thereby avoiding the expensive problems of private detectives, attorneys, and alimony.

In swapping couples, there is almost always a dominant partner—one who enjoys swapping more than the other. It's not always the man: I've known husbands who would have been quite content to stay at home and sit with their feet up in front of the hearth, rather than be dragged off by their wives to make some coital rendezvous with an unknown pair of swappers from Sparta, Wisconsin.

If your lover or husband suggests a swapping session, it's time to examine the state of your relationship pretty closely. Swapping is not an antidote to sexual boredom: it's a symptom of it. There must be something lacking between you for him to want to go out and cold-bloodedly have sex with another girl. The thought that you're having sex with the girl's husband or lover may salve his conscience, but it won't help the basic problem.

Are you being creative enough in your sex life? Or have you allowed it to become a routine? Are you doing the same old things over and over? In a long-term relationship, you can't expect the erotic freshness and thrill to remain as spine-tingling as it was in the first few weeks. But if you *work* at keeping it alive, then there is no reason why you should both drift apart, physically, through tedium and lack of inspiration. When you try to find out what's wrong, it's worth being harsh with yourself and harsh with him. It's no good traipsing off to a swinging session in the hope that a little extramarital activity will magically put things right. It won't. All that will happen will be that one or other of you, or both, will rediscover that spine-tingling feeling with someone else, and that will be the beginning of the end.

A constant search for sexual excitement with new people is doomed to lifelong failure. The excitement

group sex, and you will hopefully discover that all the variations in taste and technique and experience are to be found within your two loving selves.

# 19.

## What Does Your Lover Expect of You?

"Let those who never tried, believe
    In woman's chastity!
Let her who ne'er was asked, receive
    The praise of modesty!"
                —Anonymous, 19th century

It's often hard for a woman to work out just what it is that a man wants from her. And that's not surprising, because what men want from women is as varied as their personality, as their mood, as their sexual and social needs.

To be a perfect partner, and to make your sexual relationships work, it's essential for you to have some understanding of the paradoxical nature of men's sexual desires (just as it's equally important for *them* to comprehend yours).

Despite their physical dominance, men are frequently weaker and less self-contained as human beings than women. They have a deep-seated need for reassurance, praise, support and comfort. There are men who are totally self-sufficient, and can live just as well without a woman in their lives as they can with one, but they are rarer than snowflakes in August. Most men *need* a woman around.

First, and most obviously, your lover is attracted to

you because you stir his sexual lust. But it's interesting to analyze *why* you do. It may be that you have an exceptionally beautiful face, or you have a noticeable pair of 42C's. He may desire you because you're classically and traditionally desirable, and he enjoys not only being with you but showing you off to his friends.

But most men are attracted to a particular physical type of woman. If you study divorce reports in newspapers, it is remarkable how often the photographs of the deserted wife and the newly acquired mistress resemble each other. Some evening, ask your lover which female movie stars turn him on the most, and compare their facial and physical characteristics with yours. All right, they might look more glamorous and expensively dressed, but check out their eyes, their cheekbones, their mouths and their figures. If there's a distinct likeness, then you know that you're probably his physical type.

Psychologists can tell quite a lot about a man's personality from the people he finds physically attractive. Some years ago, a research psychologist called Szondi devised a test in which subjects were shown a series of photographs of various people, and asked which of them they would prefer to sit next to on a train journey, and which they would least like to be alone with. The photographs, unknown to the subjects, were all of mental patients: homosexuals, catatonics, schizophrenics and sadists. By finding out which of these the subjects felt rapport with, and which they regarded with revulsion, psychologists were able to draw important conclusions about their subjects' personalities.

If you're *not* obviously his physical type, don't worry about it too much. But if you want to keep him, file away somewhere in the back of your mind just what sort of women he seems to prefer, and scratch their eyes out when they appear on the horizon. Or at the very least, be aware of the effect they might be having on him.

Apart from facial characteristics, a man's sexual opinion of you can be quite disproportionately affected by your hair, or your skin, or your breasts, or a particular way you walk. Although I'm not sugesting that you should always try and look the way you looked when he first met you, it's worth discovering whether there's any one thing about you that puts the icing on the cake for him. One man I knew was really turned off when his wife started doing her hair in a French bun. She thought it was elegant, but he badly missed the long, wild flowing look which she used to have before. It might sound petty, but sexual attraction is made up of all sorts of petty details and happenstance.

How much sexual attraction for him does your lover expect you to show? It depends very much on his age and his personality. Many men are very embarrassed about being kissed and cuddled in public, while others relish it. On the whole, be discreet about it, but show that he obviously turns you on. When he kisses you goodbye in his car, give him a quick and affectionate fondle between the legs as well. When you're at a party with him, don't forget to tell him he's the sexiest guy there. When he introduces you to his friends, he'll appreciate it if you take his arm and show by your smile and your affection that you're fond of him.

How obviously sexy does he expect you to dress and behave? Again, this will vary according to age-group and personal character. I knew a porno magazine publisher in his late forties who always wanted his girlfriend to walk around in the shortest possible skirts, with no panties underneath, even in the middle of a Scandinavian winter. And he wasn't at all put out, in fact he was *pleased*, when one of her bare and ample breasts would accidentally slip out from her tiny bikini tops. He was the kind of man who needed to impress others all the time to reassure himself of his identity: and by dangling the obvious sexiness of his girlfriend in front of other men he was saying "Look what I've got and you can't have."

At the other extreme, there are men who are so possessive and jealous that they will become furious if you so much as go out for the evening in a dress that shows a hint of cleavage.

Both types are fundamentally insecure, and if you

love them and want to keep them, you will have to try and show them that you're not about to go trolling off with any man who catches your eye. You will have to make an exaggerated show of faithfulness and devotion, which may be a pain in the ass sometimes, but is the only way to convince them that you're not about to betray them.

Be very wary in your relationships with men who show these characteristics. They're the type of men who want to feel that they *own* their women, and they will often give you less credit for your individuality and personality than you deserve. They may also become violent if you make them feel too insecure. Violence is one way in which a man who feels inadequate can impress his dominance on you, and you'll have to decide for yourself whether your assertion of independence is worth a couple of black eyes.

The tragic thing about relationships in which the man is very weak and insecure is that women will often nag and provoke their lovers into showing some strength and guts, even when they know very well that the only way in which the man is capable of doing this is by hitting them. That's why so many affairs and marriages in which there is constant violence go on for so long: even though she's been beaten, the woman will feel that at least her man has done *something* to assert his masculinity and his attractiveness. But these relationships are a dead end. The more he hits you, the guiltier and more insecure he will feel, and after that there's only one possible solution: break it off, for ever.

With a normal, reasonably secure man, you can be sexy and flirtatious, and he'll like you for it. Every man wants to think that his woman is attractive to other men, as long as you're unequivocal in the way you demonstrate your love for him. You can tease your lover about your attraction to other men just so far, and then it's time to stop. Masculine pride is a touchy, volatile commodity.

Your lover expects you to be good in bed, and responsive to his lovemaking, and he will appreciate any creativity you can bring to your sex-life. But tread cautiously when you compare his sexual performance, even if you're praising it, with the performance of other men you've had. You can tell him he has the best and biggest cock you've ever known, but don't persist in talking about previous lovers. Just think how you'd feel if he kept comparing you to his previous girlfriends. If you want to make a suggestion to him that you think will improve his ability to arouse you, don't ever say that, "Mike used to have this way of tickling my tits . . ."

Apart from sex, what does he want from you?

He wants you to encourage him in whatever work he's engaged in, and show an interest in it. If you happen to be dating a research biochemist, you may be in trouble stifling the yawns, but persist in trying to get him to explain it to you in simple terms. Listen when he rants on about office politics, because they're the stuff of his daily life, and he may not have anyone else to discuss them with.

If he's married, he may also want you as a friend. This may sound paradoxical, but many men, once they are married, find it difficult to keep up intimate friendships with women. Apart from the fact that they may not have the time, most of the girls they do meet socially tend to be married like themselves, and so both of them are more likely to observe the taboos and proprieties of wedlock and stay at a respectful distance from each other. Wives (and husbands, for that matter) always think the worst.

In some cases, your lover may even want you as a mother. There are times when even the strongest and most dominant men feel helpless and defenseless and women have a particular facility for soothing them, looking after them, and helping them to reorient themselves. There are also those little tasks like sewing on buttons, cooking a decent meal and doing the shopping, which some perfectly intelligent men seem to be incapable of coping with.

How much of a mother you're prepared to be is something you'll have to decide for yourself. But beware of the man who seems to want constant coddling. His love is immature, and if the time arises when you have to depend on it, you may find it lacking.

Very few men are so self-absorbed that they can go through the whole of their lives working and striving for their own satisfaction alone. You, as his lover, can help him enjoy the fruits of what he does, by showing your appreciation when he achieves something worthwhile, and by helping him celebrate. What's the good of pulling off a tremendous sales deal, or writing a best-selling book, if you don't have a woman to go home and tell all about it? In the same way, you can broaden his outlook and deepen your relationship by telling him what you've done and thought during the day.

As a mistress, and especially as the mistress of a married man, you will need considerable strength. If he's started a relationship with you because his marriage is tiring and boring and breaking apart, the last thing he'll want or expect from you is more difficulty and more problems. Because if you're too much trouble, he may well decide that the security of his married life, no matter how dismal it has become, is easier than going through with a fretful and traumatic affair. His wife has most of the odds in her favor: his house, his children, his respectability, and those are not easy odds for you to fight. He will expect of you the things he doesn't have in his marriage, and if you can't provide them, you are definitely running a losing race.

These are just some of the things that your lover will expect from you. What, in return, should you expect from him?

When you love a man, that's a difficult question to answer. Some women will put up with almost any kind of indignity to keep the man they want. You've probably done things yourself that make you blush when you think about them: begged and pleaded when you promised yourself you would never beg or plead. Given him chances when you knew damn well that he didn't deserve a chance. Tolerated indifference and anger and lack of consideration.

But it's important for your lover, as well as yourself, that you try and make sure that your relationship is not just a one-way affair.

Tell him if he's not showing you the attention and affection you need. Tell him if he's treating you more like a possession than an individual. Tell him if your sex life is growing stale. You can't basically change anyone's character, but many men need the occasional sharp reminder not to let their relationships slip. If he expects you to stay around, and be his lover and confidante and mother and wife and whatever else he needs, then it's up to him to make life enjoyable and stimulating and pleasant for you. There's no point in being a mistress at all if you're miserable.

The worst situation of all is when you allow a failing relationship to drag on, just because it's easier and you're afraid of being without him, even though you're unhappy when you're with him. Then is the time to expect him to come up with the goodies, or quit. It may be painful and distressing but in the end it's the only realistic alternative.

A perfect mistress can only be perfect when she has the right man to exercise her talents with. Whatever he expects of you, you have the right to expect him to be a lover who's worthy of the name.

# 20.

## *How to Tease and Please Him*

"Sometimes, just to excite him and turn him on, I go to a party without any panties on. Then when he's talking to some other woman, or he's right in the middle of a serious conversation with some friends of his, I check that nobody's looking my way except him, and I lift up my dress. He can never resist it. At the end of the evening he takes me home, and he usually has his pants open and starts fucking me the moment we've closed the front door, with my dress up around my hips and my shoes still on.

That's 24-year-old Debbie talking—a young New York girl who's found that shock tactics can inject regular mainline highs into her sex life. As we've seen, men are very responsive to *visual* sex, and anything you can do to dangle your metaphorical carrot in front of him will set his adrenalin going. Whatever you think about men's magazines with their nude and busty models, and whatever you think about striptease and topless bars, they are there because they make money, and they make money because men are excited by them. The lesson, as far as the titillation of your own man is concerned, is an obvious one.

Tempting him sexually in places where he finds it difficult to do anything about it is a favorite tactic. The more public or offbeat the location, the more likely you are to arouse him. This is Sue, a 23-year-old Los Angeles secretary, describing her own preferred technique.

"I have a beautiful pair of black velvet culottes, and I sometimes wear them when we're out doing our weekend marketing, or maybe when we're just driving around town in the car. Usually I wear panties under the culottes, but occasionally I kind of *forget*, you see, and either I tell him when we're far enough away from home not to turn back—you know, something like 'Oh God, I forgot to put any panties on!' or else I just kiss him and say that I've left them off.

"I don't know what it is, but the idea of that really turns him on. He's always feeling my ass, and trying to slip his hand up the leg of my culottes. I remember one time I didn't tell him, and we were out driving to see some friends in the suburbs. As we were driving along, I just raised one leg up on the seat, and of course the leg of my culottes fell back, and when he looked across at me, he could see the inside of my thigh, I guess, and a little fringe of pubic hair at the side. He almost swerved off the road.

"He kept on driving with his left hand on the wheel, but he slid his other hand over and into the leg of my culottes, and he started stroking my cunt, and finally he managed to work his finger inside. I was as excited as he was, and I held his hand against me, and gripped it between my thighs, and in the end I took hold of his wrist and moved his hand up and down against my clitoris.

"You couldn't have heard anything in the car except us breathing hard, and the wet sound of his hand rubbing my cunt. My clitoris seemed to rise up as hard as a little bird's beak, and there were *waves* of sexy feeling flowing right through my cunt and my thighs.

"All the time there were cars driving by on both sides of us, and nobody even guessed that he had his hand inside my pants and that he was bringing me off like that. He said, 'I want to fuck you—where shall we go?' but I said, 'There isn't any place at all—not on this road,' and that's why I'd chosen it, because he *couldn't* fuck me. I was teasing him and he couldn't fuck me, and that made my teasing ten times as tantalizing.

"His finger rubbed my clitoris harder and quicker, and I knew I was going to come. I started to feel remote and strange, you know, and there was a tight feeling around my head, like I had a kind of headband on. My whole cunt was tingling the way your feet tingle when you warm them up after a walk in the snow. Fantastic, beautiful. I could see the bulge in his pants as well, and I wondered whether he would cream in his shorts, just spontaneously, like that.

"I started to think dirtier and dirtier thoughts. I lay back on the seat and closed my eyes and thought of being fucked right then and there, and I pictured his big hard cock disappearing down into my pubic hair, and then I was praying that he wouldn't stop rubbing me with his finger because my clitoris felt huge—it felt as big as the whole world. Then the whole world just went kabloooooomm, and I squeezed his hand up against my cunt, and I had an incredible orgasm right there on the car seat.

"We drove along a little way further, and his right hand, you know, on the steering wheel, was still shiny with the juice from my cunt, and I could smell the smell of my own cunt in the car. It was a beautiful, sexy smell. He knew I wasn't going to do anything for him in return, not just then, and I guess his balls must've felt as tense and cramful as a chipmunk's cheeks. But he turned round and he looked at me, and he said, 'If there's one picture of you I'll always remember—it's you sitting there with that big fat smile on your face, and that drop of cunt juice running down your leg from the inside of those goddam pants.' "

Well, that's one way of doing it. But you don't have to skip around without panties to arouse the man in your life. You can be a little more subtle, and subtle teasing is sometimes more effective than blatant teasing.

Think of erotic teasing as a movie preview clip—a little taste of what is to come later. It will keep your man interested in you, and it will also whet his appetite for a full-scale sexual performance when circumstances allow.

You don't even have to parade your body around. As Lois, a 27-year-old stewardess, told me: "I believe that a few words are worth a thousand low-cut dresses. I think that low-cut dresses are lovely, and if you have good breasts it's wonderful to be able to walk around and watch the way that men can't help following you with their eyes. But I always use suggestive conversation to get a man going.

"I have a current steady, Allen. He's so sensitive to dirty talk that you only have to look as though you're going to start saying something sexy and he's practically on the verge of raping you. I'll tell you how I do it, though. If we're out someplace, maybe with friends or just walking or something, I suddenly start saying sexy things to him, right in the middle of an ordinary conversation.

"Like, we were sitting in a restaurant the other day,

and we were talking about some new chairs we wanted to buy for the apartment, and after Allen had kind of described to me the kind of chairs he wanted, and he said, 'What do you prefer?' I said, 'I prefer to have your lovely stiff cock in my mouth.'

"He knew I was going to start turning him on, so he tried to change the subject back to chairs, but I wouldn't. It excites me to tease him. I *looked* as though I was talking about something completely normal, and every time a waiter came close, or someone passed by on their way to another table, I started talking about chairs again, without even interrupting the flow of my voice.

"But all the time I was saying things like, 'I would love to feel your beautiful cock all the way down my throat, and your big tight balls against my lips. I'd love to suck you and lick you, and then I'd run my tongue right down between your balls, and lick and suck at your beautiful ass. Then I'd massage your cock with my hand, until that lovely clear juice came oozing out of the little hole in your cock, and I'd lick that up with the tip of my tongue. Then I'd suck you and lick you so fast and so hard that you wouldn't be able to stop yourself from coming, even if you wanted to, and when your beautiful white spunk came shooting out, I'd open my mouth and I'd swallow it right down, and then I'd kiss you all over until you went to sleep.'

"Of course, by the time I'd gone through all this, Allen was so horny that all he wanted to do was take me straight back home and go to bed. But I said I had to rush off and buy myself a blouse, and I didn't see him until the evening. Do you know, that guy was like a loaded gun. He'd been around town all day, just thinking about what I'd said to him, and boy was he ready for it. But I bet you one thing. I bet he never even glanced at another woman all afternoon. All he could think about was what I'd promised him.

"You know something, though, when you tease a boyfriend like that, you have to deliver the goods some time. Maybe you don't have to do it the same night, or even the same week. But if you promise something, I mean if you promise something sexual, you have to do it in the end.

"So when Allen came home that evening, that same evening after I'd been talking to him like that, I did just what I'd said I was going to do. And it was beautiful. You can tease a man, but I think you have to satisfy him, too. I think that's so essential."

It's true that if you want to keep your steady lover steady, then you will have to please as well as tease. But there are times when you can tease and *not* please, and that's when you're provoking other men, apart from your regular lover, with the express intention of arousing your lover's jealousy and protective instincts. If there's one thing that's *guaranteed* to make your man pay attention to you, it's the sight of another man sniffing around you with lust in his eyes and a hard-on in his pocket.

There are plenty of ways of handling a double-tease like this. But, be warned. It is a potentially high-explosive situation (that's why it works so well) and one wrong move from you could set it off prematurely. The last thing you want to be damaged in the blast is your relationship with the man you love.

Here's Polly, a 25-year-old travel bureau clerk: "I have the kind of boyfriend who spends half his time wondering if I turn on to other men, and the other half of his time wondering if other men get turned on by me. He's very jealous, which I like sometimes, but other times can be a pain in the neck. But if I ever think he's losing interest in me, even in the slightest, if I think he's not paying enough attention to me on a particular evening, then all I have to do is flirt with a couple of other men, and he's *there*, all ready to make hamburger meat out of the other men, and all ready to take me home and make violent love to me.

"I have to do it right, though, and not overkill it, because if he sees me flirting around too much, he starts blaming *me* for what's going on, instead of the other men, and that means we're going to have an evening of sulks and aggression. I don't want to make him out to sound like a spoiled kid, because he's not—he's a great guy and he loves me a lot, but sometimes he just needs prodding into showing it.

"What I usually do is flash my eyes over his shoulder at some other guy when we're dancing or talking, and try to convey the impression that I'm saying, silently of course, 'Oh God, will nobody save me from this boring, suffocating man.' So when we start circulating around the party or whatever, I track down the other guy again, and we get into conversation, and I flash my eyes again and lick my lips, and start looking all hot and bed-roomy, and of course the guy gets turned on.

"But as soon as my own boyfriend shows, I change my whole attitude straight away. I make out the other guy's bothering me, and that I'm bored stiff and trying to get away from him. So my boyfriend comes up, and gives the other guy one of his 'Beat it, creep,' expressions, and takes my arm and carries me off like a knight in shining white armor. For the rest of the evening, he's usually real nice to me, and looks after me properly, and when we get back home again, he's ready to give me a real good bout of lovemaking.

"I don't have the slightest intention of leaving him, ever, but it wouldn't do him any harm to think so."

It's not for nothing that some romantic books say that, when a man has intercourse with a woman, "he possessed her." For a man, the notion of *owning* a woman is still strong in his psyche, however primitive it may seem to be. When a man takes a woman back to bed and makes love to her, he is showing, among other things, that he possesses her. You will be able to provoke a display of possessive sex (which is as good and wholesome as any other kind, physically speaking) by showing your man from time to time that he *doesn't* own you, and that you're still just as attractive to other men as you ever were. This kind of mild flirtation has another beneficial effect, too. It will make you feel better, and remind you (if you need reminding) that you are a pretty, magnetic and stimulating young lady.

The principal object of teasing is to keep your lover's

sexual blood pressure high, and to keep his eyes on you. The best teases are the girls who understand that it doesn't pay to be too satisfied with any sexual relationship. Look around, at parties and dinners, at the men who are ignoring their wives or girlfriends, and you will see that their wives or girlfriends have grown too contented, too satisfied, and they're not fighting for their men's attentions any longer. The trouble is, the moment you stop fighting, that's the moment when his eyes will start to stray, and if you're not careful they will settle on that brown-haired girl in the corner with the tight satin dress and the big breasts.

You're entitled to feel some satisfaction and contentment within a long-term sex relationship. That's one reason, after all, that you want to stick around. But keep digging a mental pin into yourself, and don't let your attention wander away from your man and his sexual appetite. One girl I know keeps a diary with random dates circled in it throughout the year. On each of those dates, she does *something* positive to provoke her lover— whether it's masturbating him before he's fully awake in the morning, or sending him a love letter.

"Once lovers live together, they don't seem to send each other love letters any longer," she said. "That's sad, because you can say so much in a letter that may sound kind of awkward when you try to speak it. You can be much more romantic, and you can be sexier, too. Once every three or four months, I send Paul a long letter that tells him just how much I love him, and just how much he turns me on. I say all kinds of erotic things in the letter—about how my cunt is waiting for him, and how fantastic he feels when he's inside me. He sits up in bed and reads this letter, and then he turns over and shows me how much he loves me. You couldn't wish for a better start to the day than that—at least I couldn't."

When you're trying to catch a man's sexual attention, you can be as corny as you like. You can even try the old favorite standby—the bedroom striptease, complete with sleazy accompanying music on the stereo. Bump and grind and peel your clothes off for him with all the exaggerated mannerisms of a Gypsy Rose Lee. It doesn't matter if neither of you take the whole thing totally seriously, because striptease is a man-arousing formula that works. It's tried and tested, and unless you really screw it up by overbalancing when you're trying to take off your tights and falling on your ass, you'll get him going whether he likes it or not.

One of my favorite teases is what I called the "previous lover" tease. Unless your present lover is your first-ever, you will have a few sexual experiences to tell him about, and there's no quicker way to arouse a man's jealousy and possessiveness than by talking about the men who have come this way before him. You could start the conversational ball rolling by asking him about *his* previous girlfriends, and when he's finished giving you a rundown, you can start telling him about *your* previous lovers. Since he's just regaled you with the details of his own love life, he won't have a leg to stand on.

Tread carefully when you tell today's lover about yesterday's lovers. But if you handle it discreetly (i.e., if you explain that *none* of them was as good as you, darling), then you'll arouse his jealousy, and his penis, to just the right level.

"I always wanted to have Stephen go down on me and eat my pussy," said 28-year-old Shella. "But he didn't seem to like doing it, and he hardly ever did it, and the trouble was that the less he wanted to do it, the more I craved it. So in the end, I started talking about John, my previous boyfriend, and how he used to eat my pussy. I told Stephen that I used to enjoy it with John, but that John had never ever managed to make me come by eating my pussy—which actually was true.

"The first thing that Stephen did was to go down on me and eat my pussy until I had an orgasm. It was the first time that anyone had ever managed to do that to me, and I told him so. He felt that he'd gotten rid of John's ghost, if you know what I mean. Every man, because of his pride, seems to want to cancel out the memory of the guys you knew before. They can only do that by being *better*. That's why, if you want your guy to do something, then set him a target to beat. Make him feel he's done better than any other guy has ever managed to do before. But, whatever you do, tell him how good he was afterwards."

So remember the word is—*tease*. Keep your man guessing, sexually speaking. Keep him excited, keep him provoked. Keep him.

But remember to please him, too. Because there is an old Chinese proverb which says: "A dissatisfied lover is like a waiting lion. His body is here, but his mind is on future feasts."

# 21.

## *Your Breasts and What to Do About Them*

> "Long I've loved thee, darling Sarah,
> Gradually more ripe and blooming;
> Daily, hourly, plumper, fairer,
> In the swelling charms of woman."
> —"The Budding Rose," anonymous, 1890

Almost every girl I've ever met has been secretly—or not so secretly—worried about her breasts. If they're too small, she's desperate to enlarge them; if they're too big, she's concerned because they droop and she can never find pretty clothes to fit.

How much should you fret about your breasts? Does it really matter if you're flat-chested or floppy? Do men actually fall over backwards for girls with enormous bosoms?

Let me say one thing straight away: I believe that if your breasts make so much difference to a man that he wants you to alter them, then he isn't worth knowing. Women aren't passive, bovine sex objects, fattened up for the personal enjoyment of men.

But let me say something else: whatever you think about it, men do find the sight and the feel of larger breasts more directly sexually stimulating. It's a fact that's borne out by the monotonous screen and stage success of Jane Russell, Jayne Mansfield, Sophia Loren, Raquel Welch, Diana Dors, Sabrina, and Chesty Morgan. Chesty Morgan, incidentally, is the red-hot lady who is currently wowing them all over the United States with her 72-inch bust. Yes, you read that correctly—72.

And it's true, too, that many women feel more feminine with larger breasts. One girl told me: "I had always had very small breasts. When I was pregnant, my breasts of course grew much larger, and I really enjoyed having them as big as that. It made me feel more of a woman. Now I've finished breast-feeding, and they've gone back to their smaller size, I still hanker after having big ones again."

Since your sexual confidence is so closely involved with your breasts, and since sexual confidence is essential to you if you're going to become terrific in bed, it's worth examining what you can do about your bosom.

If you have naturally large breasts, spend a little time each day keeping them in shape. Each night and morning, splash them with cold water to keep the muscles taut, and before you go to bed, rub some baby lotion in them to prevent the appearance of stretch marks. It's worth taking the trouble to find bras that fit you really well, and not making do with ones that are too tight or too loose, because you'll regret it later. Try and avoid getting too fat, too, if you have a tendency to overweight. When you finally decide to slim, you may find that your breasts grow slack and out of shape.

Some girls find that if they sleep in a lightweight night bra, it makes for greater comfort in bed, and keeps their breasts in order.

If your breasts are truly enormous, and you have a real complex about them, it's possible to have them surgically reduced in size. The plastic surgeon simply makes an incision under each breast, and removes some of the spongy tissue which the breast is composed of. It costs about $2,000. On more drastic operations, it's sometimes necessary to resite the nipple further upwards. This is done by cutting it off and regrafting it a couple of inches up the breast.

But if you have large breasts, remember that there are plenty of girls who wish they had a bust like yours, and that men will look at them rather differently than you. They won't be worried that you can't wear that slim-line summer dress, or that elegant Paris suit. They'll be much more interested in what you look like as a sexy woman.

You can visually reduce your top-heaviness by wearing ankle-length or floor-length dresses, especially ones that fall from under the bust. You can wear deep-plunge necklines, but make sure they don't squash your breasts out of the opening like two steam puddings on the same plate.

If you have naturally small breasts, what you lack in voluptuousness you can more than make up for in feminine style. You can wear tantalizing shirts and blouses, open as deep as you like, with no bra underneath. You can wear really slim-fitting suits and dresses. You can emphasize your bottom and legs by wearing ultra-tight jeans and slacks. Make the most of your hair and eyes.

There are hundreds of products on the market which claim to enlarge the breasts: creams and pills and a thing like a milking machine which sprays cold water on to your bosom. You can try them if you like, but none of them have any substantial or lasting effect, and the best of them only give you an apparent bust enlargement by toning up the muscles that support your breasts, which you can do yourself for free, with regular exercise.

Think deep and hard before deciding to have surgical bust enlargement. Don't do it because you think the man in your life would be more attracted by it, but because you want to do it for the way *you* feel. He can walk out of your life next week, but your breasts are going to stay with you. Talk to your doctor about it, and give yourself plenty of time in which to change your mind.

Enlargement mammaplasty, as it's technically known, is done by two methods: implant or injection. The silicone implant is a cushion of silicone with some kind of covering which is placed between the breast and the wall of the chest. It was developed by Dr. Thomas Cronin at Baylor University in Houston, Texas, in 1963, and the implants are manufactured by Dow-Corning under the trade name Silastic, with a backing of Dacron discs which help them stick to the chest wall.

In Los Angeles, a Dr. Ashley has devised his own version, which is a silicone pad covered by polyurethane sponge with its own Y-shaped breast-bone built in. He claims this does away with the heaviness and sagging of the Cronin implant.

Breast implants come in the following sizes: mini, petite, small, small extra fill, medium, medium extra fill and large extra fill.

One doctor commented: "We're really slipping up here—nobody wants a mini or a petite. We should borrow our terminology from the detergent manufacturers and make everything giant, mammoth and super economy size."

Another doctor says his implant customers are mostly housewives: "She got her man in spite of being flat-chested, but even he, over the years, couldn't help revealing that he longed for women with larger breasts. So one day they get around to seeing me together. It's a kind of seven-year-itch present from the husband to his wife. He usually sits in the corner listening quietly until it gets to the question of size. His wife is amazed by his extravagant requirements! If we did what he wanted, she'd end up looking like Mae West."

The other method of breast enlargement—using liquid silicone injected straight into the breast—is illegal in the United States, but there are doctors who will do it anyway. Only eight U.S. plastic surgeons are licensed by the Food and Drug Administration to use injected silicone on an experimental basis only, and not in the breasts. It is mainly used to fill out facial disfigurement.

Liquid silicone is heavy and can be dangerous in the breast area, because it's impossible to feel any breast tumors through it. It has to be injected very slowly over a long period with great skill. But some illegal practitioners give huge doses only a week or two apart.

Said one specialist: "Since they can't get high-grade silicone from the FDA, the illegal practitioners get hold of it from anywhere, such as a local builder's or hardware store. So desperate are some women for impressive frontage that they'll seemingly run any risk, and put themselves in the hands of any quack. Many bypass the law by taking off for Japan, where silicone injections are widely done."

Costs of enlargement mammaplasty vary, but don't expect to have much change out of $2,500.

If you take care of your breasts, and dress to show them to their best advantage, there's no reason why the ones you already have shouldn't make you as attractive and sexy to your lover as the ones you *wished* you had. You might console yourself with the thought that many men wish they had much bigger penises, and use all kinds of strange devices, including massagers and vacuum pumps, in order to gain another eighth of an inch.

# 22.

## *Perfect Mistresses on Perfect Mistresses*

What do women who have been mistresses themselves think a perfect mistress should be?

I talked to three girls from different social backgrounds, all of whom had been involved in different kinds of affairs. I asked them to define, as clearly as they could, the role of the perfect mistress, and how they thought a woman could learn to become one.

Here's Marise, a 26-year-old housewife, who had a three-month affair with a friend of her husband while her husband, Anthony, was away on a European business trip:

"As a mistress, I think I was far from perfect to begin with. I was so frightened that I was going to be discovered that I did everything in a blue funk. I'm surprised Anthony even wanted to go on with me, but in the end I began to realize that I had just as much responsibility to make our relationship work as he did, and things started getting better then. In fact, they got so much better that we realized we had to make the decision either I left Michael, or we would have to break up.

"It started in such a peculiar way. I always give myself the excuse that I was unprepared for it, and that's why I made such a mess of things. But it never used to be like that before I was married. I had four quite long affairs with men before I met Michael, and all of those were pretty calm and reasonable and successful. It was just the stresses and strains of having an affair when I was married. I wanted to do it, but at the same time I couldn't help feeling terribly guilty.

"Anthony came around one afternoon when I was watching television and asked whether he could borrow Michael's power drill. I said that was fine, and got it out for him, and then he stayed for a cup of coffee, and I told him that I was getting pretty lonely all by myself in the house. So he asked me whether Michael would mind if I went out for dinner with him that evening. I thought about it, and thought, well, why not? Michael's probably out enjoying himself somewhere, so why shouldn't I? It truly didn't occur to me that we would sleep together or anything like that.

"Anthony came around in the evening and took me out to dinner, and I really enjoyed myself. I began to feel that wonderful warm self-satisfaction that you feel when you know someone finds you attractive, and being married I hadn't felt that for ages and ages. We had quite a lot of wine to drink, and by the time Anthony drove me back home, we were laughing and carrying on like a couple of kids.

"He came in for a last drink, and we sat on the settee together, and then he leaned over and started stroking my hair. 'That's nice,' I said. And it was nice. Then he leaned over a little more and kissed me. 'That's even nicer,' I said. And then we really started kissing. I didn't protest or object or anything. I didn't feel any guilt then—only excitement. Anthony is really quite attractive, and the feeling of having another man kissing me and wanting me like that was tremendous.

"He unbuttoned my dress at the back, and took it off my shoulders, and then he put his hand inside and fondled my breasts. The feeling of another man's hands, after all that time! The blood was absolutely rushing around my head, and my panties were soaking. I put my hand down and felt his hard-on through his pants, and it seemed so stiff and sexy.

"We made love on the carpet, there and then. I just lifted up my dress and he got on top of me and fucked me. I can remember, just as his cock was about to go inside me: *another man's cock, I'm married but I'm having another man's cock in me*. I had forgotten how sexy sex could be. I could smell his aftershave and feel his muscles, and his fantastic hard cock going in and out of me, and I had such an orgasm, you wouldn't believe it. I lay there trembling afterward.

"In a way, I felt relieved when it was over because I'd gotten rid of my sexual frustration, and also because I felt that this would be the only time. Just once, and then never again. I'd committed adultery, but it would be something I could wipe out of my mind. But Anthony wanted to see me again, and I couldn't resist. I called him up two or three times to put him off, because I was scared of what might happen, but each time I was weak enough to let him persuade me to go on with it. We met the next time about a week later, and we had an argument about sex. Of course he thought that because he'd made love to me once, he could do it again. I told him I'd changed my mind and couldn't. I didn't mind going out with him, or having him around, but I couldn't keep on going to bed with him.

"That was where I *wasn't* being a perfect mistress. I did, in fact, want to be his mistress. But at the same time I wasn't prepared to take the risks that being his mistress would have involved. The trouble was, I didn't end it then and there. I made it clear to him that if he tried hard enough, and maneuvered me hard enough, he could have me.

"He stayed that night, in the end, and after that we saw each other at least three times a week. Every time we had the same wrangle and the same argument. After a while, I knew I was going to lose him. I could sense it, in the way he started to act and talk to me. I felt partly relieved because it would mean that he took the responsibility of ending it, which I didn't have the nerve to do; and I felt partly upset because I didn't want it to end. You can judge the state of mind I was in.

"I went away and stayed with a girlfriend of mine for the weekend, and talked it over with her. She said that I should do whatever I really wanted to do, and that if I *did* want Anthony, I should go into the affair with a whole heart, rather than mess around feeling guilty and depressed. She said if I wanted to do it, I should give it a real try.

"So that, in the end, was what I decided to do. Instead of thinking about myself and my problems so much I began to think about Anthony. I don't really think I'd thought about him as a *person* up until then, only as my illicit lover. I began to think, well, what does *he* want out of it? Does he love me, or what? What can I do for *him*?

"It struck me that he was really quite a lonely sort of man, and that he enjoyed our relationship as much for the friendship it gave him as for the sex. So the next time I saw him, I started taking an active interest in what he had to say, and what he'd been doing, and even though it was an effort at first, I found that after a while I really was interested in him, and that he was responding to my interest. We made love that night in quite a different way. We weren't just thinking about having a quick fuck to satisfy our appetites—or at least, I wasn't. We made love because it expressed the way we felt about each other. It was long and slow and lovely, and even though I wasn't so excited by the idea of making love to anothe rman, I think I was more excited by the idea of making love to *him,* if you can understand what I mean.

"Our sex relationship got better and better as well. Once I'd started being interested in him for what he was, I started being more interested in what I could do for him, rather than what he was doing for me. I wanted to try out new sex things with him, things that Michael and I hadn't done. One night he fucked my bottom, and that was the first time anyone had ever done it. It was the first time I'd ever wanted anyone to do it. I began to find out that it isn't what you know about sex, or what you can do as far as sort of *technique* is concerned, it's what your emotional relationship with your lover leads you to do naturally. You start doing things not because you feel you ought to, but because you want to.

"I think that's what being a perfect mistress is. I mean, I think it's important, if you're going to have a good affair, for the man to feel the same way about you. But he's more likely to feel like that if you stop worrying about yourself, and start thinking about what you can do to give him pleasure, and what you can do to make him feel wanted and loved and good.

"As it turned out, we decided the week before Michael came back that we'd have to finish. It was very painful, and I still haven't quite got over it. But what I learned with Anthony, I've tried to do with Michael as well, and I certainly think our marriage is a lot better for it."

As a contrast, this is Anita, 28, a photographer's model who has had, by her own reckoning "at least fifty affairs":

"The trouble with sex is that you can go on for years thinking you know it all, and suddenly you come across someone who makes you realize you don't know very much at all. But I think what makes a mistress perfect—and makes a lover perfect as well—is a willingness, you know, to *respond* to what the other person wants.

"I had my first affair—well, it wasn't really an affair, it was more like playing doctors and nurses—when I was 14. I really swooned over this boy—Sam, I think his name was. I don't think he was all that interested in girls, though, he was more interested in baseball. We kissed with our mouths closed, and then one day we were alone in his house, and he showed me his dick, and we did it. I was heartbroken when he said he didn't want to see me anymore—this was about two weeks later. But I think what was good about losing my virginity like that was that it never got in my way again. I lost it so young that I could never make a fetish out of it.

"I know fifty affairs sounds impressive, but very few of them actually were. Most of them happened when I was at college, with undergraduates. I can't remember all of them. I think most of my girlfriends thought I was very sexy—and loose. I suppose I was in a way. But I found that if boys thought they could sleep with me, they'd all want to know me, and be nice to me, and to tell you the truth I was rather lonely.

"I don't think I was very good in bed because none of the boys I slept with were very good. A lot of them came as soon as they stuck themselves in me. You know, over-excitement. I used to have orgasms, but I did it *myself*, by rubbing myself against them, so in a way it was much more like masturbation than anything else. I never knew what it was like actually to think more about the guy, and what he was feeling, than about the sort of feeling I was getting myself.

"Two guys changed all that. You see, that's why I think you can't be a perfect mistress until you have a reasonable lover to practice on. You can do a lot to change a guy once you know what to do, but I never knew what to do because nobody ever told me. I didn't *know* about things like kinky sex or how to make men get erections. Girls just aren't told things like that.

"The first guy was Aaron. He worked on Wall Street in some incredibly cut-throat finance firm. He used to tell me he was employed to lift the wallets out of the other executives' pockets before they jumped off the window-ledge. I thought he was very cynical when I first met him, but you often find that guys who are very cyni-cal are only covering up their softness and their niceness.

"I met him at a party out on Long Island, some week-end birthday affair. I'd just finished with some boring guy from some boring advertising agency, and I was on the hunt. I wore my red satin dress with the cleavage that goes down to my navel, and I'd spent all afternoon at the hairdresser. I saw Aaron with some other girl, and I liked the look of him, so I zeroed in on him. This other girl was trying to get him to recommend some good shares for her to invest in. I think she thought she was being interesting, just because he was in finance. So I swept in and said to him: 'Are there still just as many hookers around Wall Street?' And after that, the conver-sation was definitely mine. The other girl faded away with some used car salesman, and Aaron and I got it to-gether.

"The party didn't finish until two or three in the morning, and then Aaron offered to drive me home. I said: 'Yours or mine?' And he said: 'Mine, of course.' He had a really neat apartment somewhere in the East 50s, 57th I think. Very tasteful, you know. Full of art. I suddenly began to realize that he wasn't like the ordinary kind of guy I'd been dating up until then.

"He undressed me, and stripped himself, and we climbed on to the bed, and I knew I was in for something different. You know, most guys, they leap on top of you like a tiger that hasn't been fed for three weeks. But Aaron spent a lot of time kissing me, and touching my breasts, and then he went down on me. I couldn't believe it. I mean, guys had gone down on me before, but the way he did it was fantastic. He did it just like it was part of everything that was going on—I mean, he didn't make a big deal out of it. I could feel his tongue lapping against my pussy, and I started to get really *turned on*. For the first time. I was really *turned on*.

"Then I thought, Jesus, he's doing all this to me, what am I doing just lying here? So I started to stroke his hair, and when he'd finished eating me, and he came up for air, I started rubbing his dick for him, and then I went down on him. I don't think I did it very well, but he kind of held my head with his hands and showed me. With any other guy, I think I might've objected, but it was so obvious that he knew what he was doing that I didn't mind.

"By the time he was ready to get into me, I was absolutely panting for it. And what was nicer, for me, was that he was panting for it too. I could feel his come sliding up inside me like—what? Like the mercury going up a thermometer, that's what it was like. At first I just lay back and tried to think about the things I usually thought about—the things that helped me to have an orgasm. But the way he was holding me and screwing me was so nice and kind of rhythmical, that I couldn't concentrate on myself, and I started screwing *him*. I moved my hips up and down and really got into *him*. I pushed myself down so his dick would go in as far as it could, and it touched me right up inside. I almost felt it was going to come out of my mouth.

"I didn't realize I was going to have an orgasm until I started shaking, and then I shook and shook and shook, and I was clinging on to him just to try and keep me still, and right in the middle of my orgasm, he came as well, and the feel of his come just blew my . . . *mind*.

"That was when I really understood what sex was all about, I mean as far as what a woman is supposed to do. It was like, you know, Saul with the scales coming off his eyes. The thing with Aaron lasted longer than any affair I'd ever had, and when it was over, I didn't feel any frustration about him, just a bit sad. We really weren't the right type for each other, but that was okay, at least we'd enjoyed ourselves.

"About two months later I met Bill, and I'm still going out with Bill. He's different from Aaron, he's not quite as gentle, but he still gets me going, he still does things to me. It's made me understand that you don't just lie there and think your own thoughts, and worry about whether *you're* going to make it or not. That's what I think a perfect mistress is—a girl who can forget about what she's getting, and give. Because when you do that you get it anyway."

Thirty-year-old Candice, a personal assistant in a large media and TV corporation, has an even wider view of the role of the perfect mistress:

"I've been married once, for six years, and it wasn't ultimately successful. Gordon was a A-1 male chauvinist pig for a start, and wouldn't lift a finger to help me in the house, and would certainly never lift his penis to help me in bed. As far as he was concerned, it was a man's world, and women were simply there to iron his fucking shirts.

"I appreciate now just how rotten Gordon was sexually, but I wouldn't lay the blame entirely on him. I don't think it's fair to do that. I think men get more sex education than women, but I don't think that either men or women get enough sex education about what they're supposed to do *together*. I learned about the reproduction of amoebas and rabbits at school, and that was the sum total of my preparation for married life. I guess it would have been okay if I was going to marry an amoeba or a rabbit, but as it turned out, I married a man.

"But if you're talking about what makes a perfect mistress, I don't think you can talk exclusively about sex. Obviously a mistress is there for sex, but since I've been having an affair with my boss, Edgar, I'm beginning to know that a perfect mistress has to be so much more than a bedmate. The way I see it, a mistress has to supply everything that a man doesn't normally get from his wife, if he's married, or out of his job and his usual girlfriends.

"It's harder than being a wife, because when you're a wife, you can relax a little. Maybe you shouldn't, but you feel you've got your man, and you don't want to have to go *on* seducing him, night after night after night. But that's why men go after mistresses. They want someone who's always sexy, who never looks harassed or tired or walks around with rollers in her hair. I know that sounds kind of *unfair,* and there are times when you think, fuck it, I've got to dress up for that guy again, even though I have a splitting headache and I'd much rather put on a crummy old dressing-gown and go to bed with a cup of hot chocolate.

"But it works both ways, you know. The guy makes an extra effort with you, too. He always turns up shaved and well-dressed, and he brings you presents and flowers, and even though you sometimes look at yourself in the glass and think 'Where the fuck am I going and what's happening to me?' there's still quite a lot of glamour in being a mistress.

"There's something else that a mistress ought to be, too, apart from a very good bedmate. She ought to involve herself in a man's work and interests, and help him to be himself. Edgar is quite powerful in the corporation, and he makes a great deal of money, but you'd be surprised how often he needs someone to talk to, someone who isn't involved in all the wheeling and dealing that goes on a big place like ours. And he needs someone he can take to company socials, someone who looks good and gives him moral support.

"I don't think there's anything to be ashamed of in being a perfect mistress, no. I know some of my friends think I ought to be more liberated and more independent, and they believe that I'm just Edgar's little kept woman. But men are men and women are women, and they have to—well, how can I put it—they have to live together, they have to *interact*. I know I'm not just a sex object to Edgar. He needs someone like me, and I need someone like him. I think it's beautiful the way women supply the mental things that men lack, and men supply the mental things that women lack.

"I've seen so many relationships where the only time that the man and the woman really come in contact is in bed, and then once it's all over, they go on living their separate lives, physically as well as mentally. I think a perfect mistress is a woman who can be a mistress all the time, not just on Thursday nights, or Saturday afternoons, or whenever you have sex. The marvelous thing about being a mistress is that you can be a *friend* as well, which a whole lot of wives just find they cannot be. They have too much of a stake in the man staying with them and supporting them to be really honest and come out and say what they truly think.

"I enjoy sex, I really do. And I think that Edgar and I have built our sex life up beautifully. Mostly we keep it out of the office, but there's something I do which really turns him on. When I go into his office to give him his mail or something, I'll quickly lift my skirt at the front and I'll show him that I'm not wearing any panties. Then just as quickly I'll put it down again. Or sometimes I'll open my blouse and give him a quick flash of my bare breast. It's a game, and it's fun, and it makes us both feel that we're sexually attractive to each other all the time.

"Edgar has taught me to be much more considerate in bed. Sometimes he's a little too much like a schoolmaster, but I love it when he puts on this serious voice and says, 'We just didn't manage that rhythm properly that time.' It's true, we didn't, and I'm glad he's said it, because next time we'll get it right, but it still makes me laugh. Edgar's truly beautiful. He's the kind of guy that I can be a perfect mistress with."

Out of all these three accounts, the point that comes over the most is *consideration*. To begin with, all of these women tended to see sex from their own point of view, as something that gave them pleasure, without really comprehending that erotic satisfaction (to coin a phrase) is a *joint effort*.

I believe that many men are guilty of the same way of thinking. But these experiences show that either partner can grow to understand the importance of being creatively considerate in bed, if it's demonstrated to them. The things you have learned in this book will help you to take the initiative with an inconsiderate man, and awaken his understanding to the importance of thinking about *you* just as much as himself. Being a perfect mistress does have its dividends.

It's interesting, too, how much a happy and constructive sex relationship can affect your whole outlook on life. English sex specialists have recently reported that in cases where they have been able to improve a couple's sex relationship, the financial and career success of both partners has been dramatically bettered.

So even if you don't think you owe it to yourself to be a perfect mistress, or to your lover, you at least owe it to your pocketbook.

# 23.

## *Games People Play*

"She giggled and she winc'd about,
But liked the picked rudeness;
She eyes me kindly—she no doubt
Remembers all my lewdness."
—Anonymous, 19th century

Late in 1974, English newspapers were full of the exploits of the bottom-smacking squire. Lieutenant-colonel John Elliott Brooks, a 64-year-old London solicitor, admitted during a libel trial that he enjoyed spanking young girls, and used to pay them to come aboard his private boat, without tights or panties on, for a session of playful smacks.

"Every healthy, normal, vigorous male is a bottom-slapper in mind if not in deed," Mr. Brooks told the judge. "I think that spanking a girl's bottom if she is willing and likes it and enjoys it, is simply a part of the fun."

All of us, men and women, have erotic fantasies. Some are stronger and more compulsive than others, but they frequently affect the way we make love, and if we play them out to the full, they become elaborate sexual games.

If a man wants to play erotic games with you, what do you do? Do you gulp, swallow your inhibitions and dive in, or do you refuse and walk off in a huff?

It depends, of course, on what the games are. If he

has torture or whipping in mind, the best thing to do is make quickly for the nearest exit. But if it's bottom-slapping games, or slave-and-master games, or French maid games, then there's no reason why you shouldn't participate and get a great deal of amusement out of them. What Mr. Brooks said is true: "It's simply part of the fun."

Although sex has its serious side, it's also very important that you see the amusing side of it as well. When you're both naked, there's no need to stand on ceremony. You don't need to have any reserve or hang-ups. You can do whatever takes your fancy, and if sex games take your fancy, then they can add a whole lot of humor and enjoyment to your relationship.

What you have to overcome is your prejudice against sex that—just because it's unusual—seems weird. Spanking girls' bottoms may seem bizarre and kinky, but judging from the enormous correspondence I used to receive at *Penthouse* about it, thousands of men and women enjoy it, and use it regularly as part of their normal sex lives.

One American woman told me: "The first time my husband spanked me was when I refused to go to a company dance with him. I said I thought the occasions were a real drag, and I'd rather stay at home. He said it was important for him that I went, and that he would lose face if I didn't. Everybody would think that I just wasn't interested in what he did.

"We started shouting at each other, and then he lifted me up, put me over his knee, raised my dress and pulled down my pantyhose and panties and slapped me, harder and harder, until my bottom was glowing red-hot. Then he threw me down on the bed. I don't know whether it was his sudden display of domination, or the actual spanking itself, but I felt, well, *aroused*. I reached out for him, and unbuckled his pants, and I found that he had a hard-on. We made love, very roughly and very passionately.

"Now, whenever I misbehave myself, he does the same thing—spanks me. And that's always a prelude to bed.

Often, I disagree with him and rile him up just to get him to do it. Spanking hurts a little at first, but then this warm tingly feeling spreads right through your bottom and your pussy, and if you ask me there's nothing like it."

Spankers usually tend to have this ritual of "misbehavior" that gives them the excuse for exercising "punishment." They also have favorite spanking instruments—like a slipper, or a paddle, or the back of a hairbrush. In some ways, there are parallels in spanking with the violence and humiliation of woman-beating, but it's obviously more controlled. If a man wants to spank you, it's unlikely that he'll want to beat you up as well.

Some spankers and spankees enjoy being "punished" in front of an audience and many of the corporal punishment letters I received at *Penthouse* described how the thrill of being spanked was heightened by the shame of knowing that other people were watching. I suspect that many of these letters were the invented fantasies of my correspondents, but several of them had the ring of truth. And whether a spanking had actually taken place or whether it was only a figment of the imagination it was still a genuine desire that the writer harbored in his or her mind.

Another sexual game that came to my attention through *Penthouse* was the practice of piercing. Some men and women enjoy having their nipples pierced, and gold rings inserted. The hobby seems relatively harmless, except if the woman later wants to breastfeed, and except if it becomes too heavily involved with bondage. Some people like to thread chains through the rings and lead their partners around like slaves on their way to the Gold Coast.

Nipples aren't the only parts of the body that get the treatment, either. In Stockholm, I saw photographs of a woman whose outer vaginal lips had been pierced to carry four rings on each side, from which depended eight small golden bells. Presumably she was the life and soul of the party at Christmas. Other women have their inner lips, the labia minora, pierced, and the rings padlocked together to form a kind of mini chastity-belt. Men don't escape, either. I have heard reports of men having their foreskins pierced with rings and locks put over their glans so that cheating, if not impossible, would at least be extremely uncomfortable.

And we mustn't forget the piercing of the septum of the nose, either. One Danish magazine carried a whole series of pictures of a girl with a bull-ring through her nose, being tugged around like livestock at the market.

If you and your lover are interested in piercing, be sensible about it. Have the infibulations done by a qualified doctor, or you could be in for a nasty infection. And don't put rings in places that you might afterward regret.

Apart from these gimmicks, many couples like to dress up and play out their sexual fantasies in the form of amateur dramatics. This can be both erotic and amusing, if you can both keep a reasonably straight face, and it can give you the chance to enact those secret daydreams that you've always thought about.

The fairest way to do it is to let *him* organize the game one night, and then for *you* to organize it on another night. That way, you both get a fair crack of the fantasy whip.

One of the favorite female fantasies seems to be that of the Eastern princess, sitting on piles of cushions amid the sensuous smell of incense, having her every whim attended to by a willing male slave. This is Tracey, talking about a sex-game that she and her lover used as a regular turn-on:

"I made myself a pair of those gauzy Oriental pants, with baggy legs to them, and gold braid round the ankles and waist. Then I put loads of jewelry on, and a silk turban with a feather in it, and sit in the living room, cross-legged on the floor. Jim has to take all his clothes off, and wear a metal choker around his neck, and he's my slave. Whatever I want him to do, he has to do. That's very important to the game. It only works if it has strict rules.

"He makes me coffee and brings me drinks. When he does that, I allow him to kiss my nipples, but he's not allowed to touch me in any other way. Then I make him do sexual things, like masturbate in front of me, and he has to catch the sperm in his hand and bring it to me so that I can taste it. Or else I make him bend over and try to fellate himself. He actually managed it once, and it looked incredible. Sometimes I lie back and make him lick me for hours. He's not allowed to stop until I tell him to. I can go on for ages like that, it's really sexy.

"None of our friends know what we do, and I don't see why they should. But it turns Jim on just as much as it does me, and when we go to bed our lovemaking is almost always fantastic."

Jack, 37, an advertising account executive, and Marcia, 32, play a different kind of game:

"We play massage parlors. I put on a yellow nylon shift over nothing at all, and I put a foam cover and a sheet over our dining table, and turn the lights down low, then Jack comes in and makes out he's a massage client. He actually has to pay me real money for everything he wants me to do, and I get to keep the money afterwards, which makes it much more real than using Monopoly money or something like that.

"If he wants a straight massage, I charge him fifteen bucks. If he wants his cock massaged, then that's ten bucks extra. Blowjobs price out at around twenty, and the whole thing costs fifty. That's what it costs in real massage parlors, so that's what I charge.

"It gives both of us a thrill, and it's funny, too, because Jack pretends to be different characters. It's sexy, and it makes us laugh, so I can't see there's any harm in it."

Some couples take their cue from Oriental sex literature. A favorite sex game is to take a copy of the erotic classic *Kama Sutra*, or *The Perfumed Garden*, and enact the erotic instructions that each one contains. Or, if you felt like it, you could take this book, and go through it from cover to cover, trying out some of the variations you've read about.

Danny, 24, and his girlfriend Madeleine, 20, enjoy a Westernized version of "yab-yums," the meditative Zen way of sex. With their apartment full of Eastern music and joss-sticks, they strip naked. Then Danny sits cross-legged on the floor, and Madeleine lowers herself carefully on to his erect penis.

"We sit like that for maybe half an hour to an hour, just digging each other, not moving, just sending out vibrations of love. Sometimes we don't come at all, but it's not the physical actions that are important. It's the love we send out to each other. Sometimes we get so involved in what we're doing that I can't work out who's Danny and who's me. It seems like we've become—well, not one person, but a higher, single, *third* being. I know we don't do it according to strict Zen principles, I mean that's not our bag, but I think that's what the Zen Buddhists were trying to get at—two people becoming something else, higher and better than both of them. And it's very sexy, too."

According to Norma Levy, the London callgirl who was implicated in the recent resignation of Lord Lambton from the British government, many men like to play games in which the girl pretends to be very much younger than she is. In other words, a legal form of Lolita-ism.

Edwina, an 18-year-old graphic designer, found that dressing as a schoolgirl did a lot for her 36-year-old lover Mark.

"He's not the kind of guy who would really chase little girls around," she said. "But I think all men are turned on by the idea of the innocent but dirty-minded little girl. I think some teenage girls are fantastically sexy. Somehow their childish clothes and everything makes them seem even more sexy.

"What Mark really likes is for me to put my hair up in pigtails, because when I do that I look about thirteen. And then I come into the bedroom wearing just a pajama top and maybe some little white panties. The other day I came in sucking a lollipop, and he thought that was beautiful. Sometimes we go out driving together and I have my hair in pigtails, and I wear long socks and a really short skirt, and Mark really likes kissing me and fondling me in front of people then. It blows their minds. They think he's a father, having an incestuous relationship with his daughter."

Some women I've talked to don't like the idea of sexual games because they think they're demeaning to their sexual dignity. I appreciate the importance of a woman's sexual integrity, and I am the first subscriber to the notion that you shouldn't sexually abuse yourself, physically or mentally. But sex is not the kind of activity that demands dignity in the way some of these women think about it. You're not sweeping down a flight of stairs at an embassy ball: you're bare naked in bed with the man you love, and the enjoyment and pleasure and fun you get out of it has its own dignity. The dignity of two people who are communicating all the affection and attraction that they have to give.

Save your stiff upper lip for society dinners and keep the fun and games going in bed.

# 24.

## *Even Further Fantasies*

Maybe the spicy food inspired it, but not long ago I found myself talking to a girl in a Greek restaurant in Manhattan, and the subject was erotic fantasies. "The trouble is," she told me seriously, "I don't *have* any erotic fantasies. Well, none that I would actually want to do for real."

She did have an idle sexual fancy of being raped by scores of savage mythical beasts, like centaurs and minotaurs and satyrs, but I had to admit that a scene like that would be rather hard to stage, at least in a SoHo bedroom.

This whole conversation set me to thinking that maybe it was about time books about sex stopped assuming that every woman is blessed (or cursed, perhaps) with a feverish sexual imagination, and that there's nothing she'd rather do than act these amazing fantasies out with the aid of her bewildered beau.

As my Greek-restaurant companion put it: "Why don't books ever give you *suggestions?* I get into bed with a guy, and my imagination goes a *blank.* I forget all the sexy thoughts I've had when I haven't been with him, and all I'm interested in is him and his cock. But I'd like to do fantasy things, if only I didn't have to think of them myself."

I talked to more women, and I found that although many of them *did* have private fantasies of their own invention which they liked to perform for real, many of them borrowed their fantasies from books they'd read, pictures they'd seen, or movies they'd visited.

So if you ever find yourself caught short for an imaginative sexy scenario with the man you love, don't hesitate to play out any erotic ideas that you've picked up from anywhere at all. He probably won't *know* that you're Scarlett O'Hara, being forcibly ravished by Civil War soldiers, but he will know that you're being extra frisky in bed tonight, and that you're giving him a lot of hot pleasure.

Susan, a 24-year-old teacher, told me that she once turned herself on so much with a "borrowed" fantasy that it has become a regular game between herself and her boyfriend.

"Did you ever see a movie called *Forbidden Planet?* It was a great science fiction movie, but the best thing in it was a robot called Robbie the Robot. He must've been about seven feet tall, and he was blue and shiny, and he had this kind of transparent plastic dome for a head, with lights going around inside it.

"What used to turn me on about that movie was when the robot picked up the girl. I've always been attracted to very hard, uncompromising men—the kind who know what they want and won't let anyone stand in their way. But think of a *robot*—you know, they're so *frightening*, because you can't appeal to their sense of pity or mercy or love or anything, because they're made out of metal.

"I can remember the first evening we got into playing this game. We'd been out together for a late dinner, and we came back to my apartment and poured ourselves drinks, and I looked around the place, and it was in a terrible mess. So I said, quite jokingly, to Mike, my boyfriend, 'I wish I had a robot to clean this place up for me.'

"He stood up and started marching around like a robot, with his legs all stiff and his arms out. He marched around the room a couple of times and I said, 'You're just like Robbie the Robot, don't attack me, I'm *frightened*.'

"Well, of course, that's exactly what he did. He came marching towards me with his arms out, and he did it so *mechanically*, knocking into chairs and things, that I really was frightened. He picked me right up in his arms and I was screaming. I was shrieking at him, 'Mike—put me down!' but he held on to me and marched me into the bedroom, and threw me down on the bed.

"I was telling him to stop it, and I know it sounds ridiculous now, but I was truly panicky, because he didn't seem to hear anything I said, and he just kept on coming with his face all set and his eyes all blank, and he gripped me so *tight*.

"He turned me over and unzipped my dress, and then he literally pulled it off me. Then he tugged off my pantyhose and my panties, and I was kicking my legs around but he wouldn't let go. I was naked then, because I don't usually wear a bra, and I knelt on the bed and pounded his chest with my fists. I was getting *hysterical*. I kept telling him to stop playing robot, but he wouldn't. He cuffed me around the head with a great big swing of his arm, and I was flung back on the bed.

"He pulled off his own clothes with really stiff movements, and he climbed on to the bed after me. I looked at his face closely to, and I said, 'Mike,' but he kept his eyes completely blank and he didn't move a muscle. I said, 'Mike, please,' but he went on acting like a robot and he forced me over on to my face. I'd never known him to be so strong. His hands were like steel, and I was genuinely frightened. I had the feeling that if I tried to struggle, he could rip me apart like wet paper.

"So he forced my head down, and he literally raped me. He pushed his cock into my cunt from the back, he rammed it straight up so that it caught my pubic hairs and really hurt. I yelped right then, but he forced me down again, and he started to fuck me, totally mechanically, in-out in-out, just the way a robot would. I kept having visions of a huge blue steel robot like Robbie, and I was *scared*.

"But he went on and on fucking me, in-out, in-out, and the feeling of that was too much. I hadn't realized how much I'd been excited by being frightened, and I almost surprised myself when I could feel my thighs starting to tremble, which is usually how an orgasm starts in me. Then the trembling seems to concentrate between my legs in a big warm sensation, and all the time Mike's metal cock was going in and out—I mean I even thought of his cock as metal. I started having convulsions in my cunt, and I knew I was just on the edge of an orgasm, but he didn't change his pace or anything. He was still sliding in and out of me at the same pace when I came, and he kept on doing it right through my orgasm, and that nearly drove me out of my head. Then he couldn't hold it any longer and he came too, and we both lay there *exhausted*. We don't play Robbie the Robot all the time, but on odd nights it's a good game. And do you know something, I'm *still* frightened by it."

That's a fantasy in which Susan's boyfriend plays an active part, but of course it's quite possible for you to play out a fantasy in your mind without your lover even realizing that you're the Queen of Sheba or Greta Garbo or Barbarella, or whoever your fantasy character is.

This kind of fantasy—the private, unshared mental daydream—is particularly useful when you find difficulty in reaching an orgasm. You may not want the man in your life to know that you have to think erotic thoughts to stimulate yourself past the point of no return—after all, it might needlessly dent that sensitive sexual ego of his. He might start wondering whether he's not arousing enough for you. Of course, he may not be, but that's a problem you'll have to look at on a long-term basis. What we're talking about is reaching a satisfying orgasm *now*.

"I used to have orgasms, but they were always so weak, and they left me feeling as though I hadn't really had one. There used to be a tremendous build-up, and I could feel the tension mounting in me, and then *pfffftttt*, it would all be over."

I've heard this complaint from girls so many times. It's what a woman writer friend of mine calls the L.M.F.—the Last Minute Fizzle. If you suffer from it, you may find that weaving yourself into a fantasy or two just before you climax will arouse you enough to keep that orgasmic sensation coming, strong and satisfying. It doesn't *always* work, but it should give you a higher orgasm count than before.

It's in this kind of self-applied sex therapy that the ready-made fantasy is particularly helpful. You don't *have* to imagine that you're being raped by Robbie the Robot. You can fantasize something like Ellen, a 22-year-old St. Louis secretary:

"You know, I used to worry about having sexy thoughts when I was making love to a man. I felt guilty about it. I used to think to myself, 'Here's this man making love to me, and I'm fantasizing about something else—what's wrong with me?'

"But then I thought, 'Damn it, he's making me have these sexy thoughts, by the things he's doing to me, and if this is the only way I can have a good orgasm, then I'm entitled to think what I like.' It made me a better lover, and because I was a better lover, my men all responded and became better lovers, too. I don't think many girls understand that nobody can be a good lover on their own, without the help of their partner.

"I've never been the imaginative kind. I guess I'm

pretty romantic, but if you asked me to think up some-thing sexy I never could. But there are things that turn me on, and I think about those when I'm making love. One thing that really turns me on is the zipless fuck idea . . . you remember in Erica Jong's book *Fear of Flying*. I think about it happening to me, about sitting at my desk and some guy walks into the room, and when he's finished his meeting with my boss he simply beckons to me and we go and meet somewhere, like a motel, and we simply fuck without every discovering each other's names.

"I've always fucked with men because I've been in-volved with them. The idea of fucking with a man be-cause I'm *not* involved with him is really sexy, I think. One of the zipless fucks I think about is the one she talks about in the train, you know. Can you imagine being in a train, and you see this fantastic-looking man sitting opposite you, and when everyone gets out of the car you simply lift up your dress and he opens his pants and you fuck.

"When my boyfriend's fucking me, and I'm getting close to an orgasm, I think of that. I imagine we're in a train, and I'm lying on the seat, and I've never seen him before and I don't know who he is. It's not hard to think that, because even when you know a man quite well, you can still look at him sometimes and think to yourself, 'That's funny . . . what's this strange man doing asleep in my bed?'

"So I think to myself that I've never met this man be-fore, and I lie there and he fucks me, and I know that I'm going to have an orgasm because this is the one and only time we're ever going to fuck. I think about how easy it would be for someone to walk in and discover us fucking in the train, and when I think about that I know I'm going to come.

"I can see the both of us in my mind's eye the way she describes it in *Fear of Flying*. Someone opening the car door, and seeing the widow in black with her dress up and her black stockings and her cunt showing, and the soldier with his pants around his ankles and his shirt tails flapping, fucking her like crazy. That's when I have a climax.

"No, I don't fantasize about things I've seen in movies, much. I can picture things I've seen in books better. I don't think I'd ever tell a man of mine about these sort of fantasies. I don't think they'd work for me any more if I did. They're something I need to help me get a good orgasm, and that's all."

Sometimes it takes even less than an obviously erotic novel to inspire a woman's sexual imagination. Kay, a 27-year-old public relations officer from New York, only has to think about one particular picture to give her orgasms the momentum they need.

"Whoever said that women don't get aroused by visual stimulus needs their head examined. There are *hundreds* of photographs that turn me on. There is one I always think of in particular. I saw it in a woman's magazine, and when I first saw it, it almost gave me a climax on the spot.

"It's a color picture. I cut it out and I've pinned it up on the inside of my closet door. Sometimes, when I'm feeling sad and blue, I go and look at it. I allow myself two minutes at a time, so it doesn't lose its freshness. And it's just so sexy that, even though it may not stop me feeling sad and blue, it still turns me on.

"It doesn't even show the man's face. It's a picture of a man's middle part, from his navel down to his knees, and he's wearing pale green satin shorts. The satin shorts are extremely tight, but he has an enormous erection, and the erection is coming down one side of his thigh, kind of strapped against his leg by his tight shorts. You can see every detail of his erection, the thick veins in it, the rim of his cock-head, and you can even see a tiny piece of purple flesh peeping from the leg of his shorts. Do you know, I think that's the most erotic picture I've ever seen, and I only have to visualize it in my mind when I'm making love, and I can *come*."

Other women imagine naked men, either "borrowed" from magazine pictures or their own experience. Some think about movie stars (Paul Newman and Steve

McQueen still get high billing in female erotic fantasies) and some think about men they've known and loved. "It's not a *crime* to be fucking one man and be thinking about another," said one girl I talked to. "If you wanted the man you were fantasizing about enough, you'd be there with *him*, instead of with the man you're with."

But without doubt, the two most popular female sex fantasies are (a) rape and (b) being watched by other people while you have intercourse. As one girl told me: "Quite often, I fantasize that my previous boyfriends are watching me while I make love to a *new* boyfriend. It's not that I really want them to be there—it's just that they're the only men I can think of. That makes me feel incredibly sexy. I could never let it happen in real life, but if I think about it when I'm making love, it makes me appreciate how good it is, the sex that I'm getting, and how much I wish I could show it off to other people. Sex is supposed to be private, and intimate, but I'm still turned on by the idea of other people seeing how well my boyfriend fucks me."

Apart from these major fantasies, here is a list of erotic scenarios, all based on popular novels or movies or other well-known sources, which will show you just how easy it is to fuel your own fantasies with borrowed ideas.

Alexandra, 25, from Boston: "There's a scene out of *Last Exit to Brooklyn*, where some whore called Tra-la-la or something gets fucked by a whole line of guys in a vacant lot. That shocked me when I first read it, but it turned me on as well. Sometimes I lie back there on the bed, and I can imagine myself as this girl, while about twenty or thirty guys line up, all holding their cocks ready, and fuck me one at a time."

Beth, 31, from New York: "My favorite fantasy is straight out of *The Happy Hooker*. I imagine that I'm a madam of a brothel, and that I'm showing all the girls in the whole place how to fuck a man properly. They're all standing around watching us while we make love, and looking really closely to see just how we do it. Whenever I have that idea, I always think of myself as a famous madam, and I can even imagine showing how to fuck on television."

Melanie, 19, from New York: "There's a scene in *Straw Dogs* I always used to fantasize about, where the girl gets raped by two men. I think I'd hate a rape if it really happened to me, but I guess when most girls fantasize about rape, they imagine they're being raped by a man they like."

Andrea, 27, from San Francisco: "I have a very strange fantasy. I've had it ever since I read *Lolita*. I like to think that I'm a very young but very sexy girl, maybe about twelve years old or so, and that I'm seducing an older man. That's what happened in *Lolita*—in the end, *she* seduced *him*, didn't she? I like to imagine I'm young and sexy, and that the man has to be so careful, because my vagina is so tight, and that I'm actually losing my virginity. I guess I must have lost my virginity a few hundred times, but the idea of it still turns me on."

Janie, 22, from Los Angeles: "There was a scene once in a movie called *Night of the Generals*. It's all about German generals in the war, and one of them is a psychopathic murderer. But the bit that I thought was incredibly erotic was when one of the generals took a girl upstairs, and he leaned against the door so that no one could come into the room, and he lifted her skirts up and he fucked her—right there, standing up against the door. I remember how she had her legs up around him, and her stocking-tops showing, and that was incredible. I sometimes hook my legs around my boyfriend's back, and I can imagine I'm that girl, sometime in the war, fucking a Nazi general up against a door."

Ella, 21, from New York: "My fantasies are always very soft and day-dreamy and romantic. I'm very big on Rhett Butler, especially when he's in one of his real masterful moods. But the thing I actually think about when I'm making love is *Last Tango in Paris*. I didn't think that was a dirty movie—I thought it was very sad and beautiful and romantic. I think about the time that Marlon Brando was making love to her, you know, from the back, with the butter. That was very sexy but it was sad as well, and somehow I find the sadness of that kind of arouses me. I think all sex is a little bit sad—that's what makes it sexy."

Fantasy has a large part to play in anyone's sex life, whether you use it privately, within your own mind, to control and stimulate your sexual responses, or whether you reveal your innermost desires to your lover so that you and he can act them out together. There's no need to worry that, because you're fantasizing, you're not being "true" to your lover, or that there's something wrong with your relationship because you're not engrossed in him alone. The erotic stimulation you feel when you fantasize may not all stem from him, but he will certainly get the benefit of it, because if you're more aroused and excited, you'll be a more passionate and adventurous bed partner.

So remember that any fantasy will do—whether it's your own, or whether it's a fantasy that you've borrowed from a book or a movie or anywhere at all. You don't have to innovate, as long as you stimulate. Nobody minds where a comedian finds his jokes, provided they make people laugh, and no man will ever object to your acting out *Last Tango in Paris* provided it gives him a good time.

And giving your man a good time, my love, is exactly what this book is all about.

# 25.

## *Seventy Sexy Things You Can Do for Him Today*

In case, after all that you've read about, your imagination ever runs short on ways and means to drive him wild in bed, here are a few dozen suggestions that should keep you going through the coming year (or even keep you coming through the coming year).

1. Wake him up at 3 A.M. and suck his penis.
2. Show him how you masturbate.
3. Borrow a Polaroid camera and take some sexy pictures of him and you together.
4. Pop a glacé cherry up your vagina and invite him to lick it out.
5. Lick him all over.
6. Greet him at the door in a G-string and quarter-cup bra.
7. Greet him at the door stark naked.
8. Shave all your pubic hair off.
9. Shave all *his* pubic hair off.
10. Ask him to show you how *he* masturbates.
11. Make love standing up in the shower.
12. Try making love in the bathtub.
13. Open his pants and start playing with him while he watches TV.
14. Insist that he makes love to you before you'll let him go to work.
15. Ring him up at the office and say suggestive things to him.
16. Tuck an explicit nude photograph of yourself into his jacket pocket, and let him discover it at work.
17. Buy him a double-ended dildo and ask him whether he has any ideas on what you could both do with it.
18. Buy a vibrator and demonstrate its effectiveness on his penis.
19. Make a plaster-cast of his penis and tell him you'll use it whenever he's away.
20. Pack an erotic letter in with his sandwiches.
21. Buy a stack of pornographic magazines and take them to bed with you.
22. Buy a vibrator and surprise him by pushing it up your own bottom while he's making love to you.
23. Buy another vibrator and surprise him even more by

    pushing the other one up *his* bottom while he's making love to you.

24. Buy him some sexy underwear—like G-strings and mini-briefs.

25. Ask him to take you to a dirty movie, strip show or topless bar.

26. Ask him to take you to a motel and register as "Mr. and Mrs. Smith."

27. Meet him from work dressed in nothing but your fur coat and boots.

28. Buy him an erotic key ring with a winged penis on it.

29. Get him to drive you out to the country and have sex in the moonlight on the grass.

30. When he comes home in the evening, massage him with scented oil, paying particular attention to his penis.

31. Read him a pornographic novel.

32. Insist that he walk around the house stark naked for a whole day, and fondle him whenever you feel like.

33. Walk around the house naked yourself for the whole day, and tell him that you're his for the taking, whenever he wants.

34. See if you can get both of his balls into your mouth at once.

35. See if he can get the whole of your vulva into his mouth at once.

36. Masturbate together, and whoever comes first wins a free dinner.

37. See how far your tongue will go up his ass.

38. Buy him some ticklers—those fancy-shaped tips to fit over the top of his penis—and insist that he demonstrate them.

39. Challenge him to make you reach an orgasm by stimulating your breasts alone.

40. Perform a striptease for him, with suitably erotic music.

41. Buy him a Medi-Stretch—a kind of strap which lashes his penis to his legs and gently masturbates

him as he walks. Then see if he isn't ready for you by evening-time.

42. Masturbate *each other* and see who can come first.
43. Masturbate him in the back of a taxi, and see if he can reach a climax by the time the meter gets to $3.50.
44. Get him to masturbate you in the back of a taxi, and see if you can reach a climax by the time the meter gets to $3.75.
45. Masturbate him in an elevator, and see if he can come by the time you reach the 50th floor. (In buildings lower than 50 floors, you're allowed to travel up and down between floors.)
46. Have a drawing contest, to see which of you can draw the most erotic picture. Then act out the winner's scenario for real.
47. Buy an inflatable sex doll each—a girl for him and a boy for you—and take them to bed for a pneumatic foursome. Dolls cost around $40 each, and these days almost all of them are equipped with oral, anal and genital facilities.
48. Try and do better than Linda Lovelace, and take your partner's penis right down your throat.
49. Let him tie you up for two hours so that you are totally helpless, and allow him to do whatever he wants to you within those two hours.
50. Tie him up for two hours (borrow a Boy Scout manual if you're not sure about the knots) and force him to submit to your wildest desires.
51. Bite his nipples so hard that he screams.
52. Play Suggestive Scrabble—no nonsexual words allowed. Winner is allowed to choose any erotic variation from the board, to be played out for real.
53. Play Guess-the-Flavors. Rub some vanilla, strawberry, mint or banana cooking flavoring on your vaginal lips, and ask him to lick'n'guess. He's not allowed to make love to you until he guesses right.
54. Go to a party without panties, and keep giving him erotic flashes up your dress.
55. Make quick and furtive love in the house of a friend

or acquaintance. Preferably someplace where discovery could be imminent.

56. Suck his penis while he's talking on the telephone to his mother or boss.

57. Ask to hold his penis while he pees.

58. Invite him to ejaculate somewhere different on you every night of the week for one week, and never the same place twice—face, breasts, tummy, thighs, feet. *Feet?*

59. Make him carry you around the room (both naked) like a horse, and whip him with a cane when he's slow.

60. Kiss him and tell him you love him.

61. Cook him a terrific dinner and serve it to him wearing nothing but stacked shoes.

62. Invite him to see how many quarters he can get inside your vagina (sterilized first, in boiling water). The rule is that you can keep as many as you can walk away with.

63. Try a new sexual position, no matter how outrageous or bizarre, every night of the week for one week.

64. If there's a lake or pool close by, go skinny dipping by moonlight.

65. Challenge him to make love to you five times in one night (but don't give him a hard time if he can't).

66. Buy him a copy of *How To Be The Perfect Lover*.

67. Ask him to buy you any item of clothing that he'd like to see you wearing, and promise to wear it. Be prepared for anything from a shred of elastic, lace and nylon, to rubber waders or scarlet silk panties.

68. Play strip checkers.

69. Tell an erotic story between you, taking it in turns to relate each incident.

70. Kiss him and *tell him you love him* again.

This is a list of suggestions that you can adopt or adapt according to your sexual tastes and your own personal circumstances. Some people hate Scrabble, so don't consider that an erotic version of this alphabetic game is obligatory. I've heard of people playing strip golf, and even strip frisbee-ing, so the possibilities are pretty limitless.

The point about all these suggestions, though, is that they are not just jokes. It's vitally important to get a real sense of surprise humor into your sexual relationships, and little gimmicks like this, tried as a treat from time to time, can add a great deal of sparkle to your erotic life. I'm not suggesting for one moment that you should do things like this every day. Your lover will begin to think he's living with a manic practical joker. But once a month, or once every two months, one of these suggestions could add some extra-special zip to your lovemaking.

They're not just designed to titillate, either. Most of them are intended to help you relax about the whole subject of sex, and to feel free and easy about telling your lover what you like and what you don't like. One of the most successful of these tips (because they've all been tried and tested for real) is the drawing contest, No. 46, which consistently produces some of the most revealing erotic fantasies that anyone's imagination could come up with. Some people draw better than others, but the wild graffiti-like result that these contests produce is invariably highly erotic.

If you have a particular favorite sexy treat which you and your lover both enjoy, I'd love to hear what it is. In my years editing various sex magazines I've learned one thing about sexual variations, and that is that no matter how fantastic and weird the erotic variations that you dream up in your mind may be, someone, somewhere, has always actually done them. And more bizarre things besides.

Above all, don't be afraid of trying games and little humorous gimmicks. They won't always work, but they will always show your lover that you think about him enough, and care about him enough, to consider just how you can surprise, please, and satisfy him.

And no one, not even a man who's accidentally pulled

out a legs-apart picture of you during an important board meeting, will ever think of you in any way but lovingly for that.

# 26.

## *Those Sad Good-byes (and Those Happy New Hallos)*

"There is not in this wide world a valley so sweet,
  As that vale where the thighs of a pretty girl meet:
  Oh, the last ray of feeling and life must depart,
  Ere the bloom of that valley shall fade from my heart."
—"The Meeting of the Waters," anonymous, 19th century

"My affair with Roger dragged on for a whole year because I couldn't bring myself to finish it. I used to sit there at work almost every day and convince myself that tonight—*tonight*—I was going to tell him it was through. But when I met him in the evening, and he started talking as though everything was still fine and wonderful, I couldn't say the words.

"In the end, I did the cruellest and most hurtful thing of all. I walked out on him and left him a note. I never saw him again, and I never saw any of our mutual friends again, either. It was a total disaster, and all because I hadn't had the guts to come out and say how I felt. What's even *worse*, and I didn't realize this until I met someone else, I had wasted a whole year of my precious life."

Breaking up, as the song says, is hard to do. And the more exciting and satisfying the affair was, the harder the breaking-up becomes. Most of the really *serious* relationship problems that I've come across are between couples who should have broken up years ago but haven't. They've fallen out of love, but they're still clinging together out of habit, possessiveness, jealousy, laziness, or even because they *enjoy* the arguments and the pain, in a masochistic kind of way.

Like anything else in life, you can be a marvelous and beautiful person, but if you put one foot wrong, you'll be remembered for your one mistake rather than for all of the good things you did. You can work for a company for ten years, being faithful and true, but on the one day you're short of car fare, and you dip your hand into the petty cash box, that record gets wiped out for ever. Whatever Nixon did in the past, right or wrong, you can sum him up in that one word "Watergate."

It's the same with your affairs. If you want to be a memorable lover, don't end your affairs with a Watergate situation. No matter how great you were in bed, no matter how affectionate and loving and romantic, your name will be m-u-d if you blow your exit.

Sometimes, pain and anguish are unavoidable. Even though you may have tired of *him*, it's possible that he may not have tired of *you*, in which case you could have a fight on your hands. When the love flame dies, smoke and tears and even the occasional fist can get in your eyes. But if you're a good enough, and a *concerned* enough, lover, you'll be able to put him down gently, and go on your way without too much recrimination.

How's it done? Well, first of all you have to understand that if you're going to be strong with him, you'll have to be twice as strong with yourself. If he still wants you, he's going to subject you to a whole battery of pleadings, cajolings, temptings and even tears. He may *order* you to stay with him, and you might laugh at the idea of that, but I've known girls whose responses are so Pavlovian that they've done just that.

Before you tell your lover that the final curtain is about to descend on your affair, sit down with yourself and a moderate number of very cold martinis, and think out the whole situation in your mind. Don't talk it over with a friend at this stage, because a friend can't help you. Only *you* can make this decision, and if you're at all reluctant about it, you will find yourself using your friend to convince you that you shouldn't take the plain but painful course that's ahead of you.

You've fallen out of love with him. Maybe it's because you've found another man who's sexier, who's better-looking, who's more your type. Maybe it's just because you've grown tired of him. You can, after all, grow tired of people, and wouldn't you expect *him* to tell *you* that he was bored, rather than keep on pretending for months and months that he loved you? Uh?

The execution itself has got to be done in cold blood. Never put yourself into a position where you can't bring yourself to let that ax fall on his neck, swiftly and cleanly, and never go back on your word once you've told him it's over.

"I made the worst mistake anyone could ever have made when I told Dennis our relationship was over," said 23-year-old Dolores, a hotel receptionist from Cleveland, Ohio. "Our affair had been running down like an old clock for months, but I was quite fond of him, and there was no real reason for breaking it up. We used to eat together, sleep together, and take in movies together, and it was good to have a friend and a companion around, even if he didn't inspire me too much.

"But one evening, Hal picked me up at the hotel. He was staying there for a week for a business convention, and he came straight up and asked if he could take me to dinner when I was through for the day. I don't know why I said yes, but he appealed to me, and I did.

"The minute I was with Hal, I literally forgot all about Dennis. Hal was everything that Dennis never could be. He was funny, he was sure of himself, and he was sexy, too. You could practically see pictures of beds in his eyes, like the cartoons. He bought me a tremendous meal, and then we went back to his hotel room, and he ordered a bottle of champagne, and he made love to me during the late movie.

"I can remember lying there on my back on the bed, and looking up into his face, and he looked so calm and masculine and sort of *in control*. I had my legs twined around his, and I could feel the hard muscles of his calves on my feet. But above everything I could feel his great hard penis inside me, and when I put my hand around and felt his balls, right up against my bottom, they were *tight*, like a clenched fist. I guess I knew right then, with Hal up inside me like that, that everything with Dennis was over. I felt an incredible sense of relief and happiness, and I was drunk, and it wasn't only the champagne that made me drunk.

"Hal shot his sperm into me, and it was like he was washing Dennis away.

"But the mistake I made—I mean, it was so crazy of me, and I just didn't *think*—was when I went home that night. I came back at about three in the morning. I hadn't told Dennis where I was. He sat up in bed all frowzy and worried about me, and I was leaping around like a Disney rabbit. I got undressed and climbed into bed with him, and he tried to put his arms around me, but I pushed him away.

"He said, 'What's the matter?' and I said, 'I've got something to tell you,' but of course the minute I said that, I didn't have to say any more, because he *knew*. You know something, he kicked me straight out of bed, and I deserved it. He was screaming at me. 'You've just come out of another man's bed, and you have the fucking nerve to get back into bed with me!'

"I packed up everything I could find, right then and there, and left. But Dennis never forgave me, and I don't see why he should. All the good times we had, I guess we both forgot about those. We did have some good times, Dennis and me, and I wish I hadn't been so stupid and ended it like that. I couldn't have been Dennis's friend, not ever, but at least he could have remembered me kindly."

It might not seem too important, to be remembered kindly by the men you've loved. But you'll discover, as time goes by, that it *is* important, both for your personal morale and for your reputation. It only takes a little thought, a little understanding, and your memory will be a fond one in the mind of almost every man you've known. That's worth something.

What Dolores should have done was to call Dennis and tell him she wouldn't be back until late. She may have been bored with him, but he loved her enough to worry about her. She should at least have done him the courtesy of letting him have a good night's sleep, and then she should have gone around in the morning, and without any hysterics, she should have told him the truth.

Never make Dolores's mistake and try to tell your lover that it's all over when you're intoxicated. You will say things that you afterwards regret, and if you get the giggles halfway through, you won't do anything but make an exhibition of yourself. *Cool*, in these situations, is paramount.

Don't telephone your good-bye, unless distance and circumstances make it essential. Don't write or telegraph. Go there in person and say your piece face-to-face, and then withdraw without argument. If you have to collect records, books and clothes, collect them all, then and there. Don't come around later and do it, or try to send someone else. Ask him if he wants any books or records back that he may have lent you, but never try to return personal gifts or jewelry, unless he has given you an engagement ring or a similar piece of expensive jewelry that was intended to be a symbol of your relationship's permanence. The law may back you up if you want to keep his $20,000 engagement ring, but your conscience won't. There was a time when it was considered part of the gamble of love, but these days it's just bad manners.

It is vital that you make your ex-lover-to-be no promises about seeing him again or reconsidering your decision. These are very hard and painful rules to keep, but when the first agony has worn off, you will find that your self-discipline repays you over and over again. If it's over, it's got to be over, and that's that.

It doesn't often happen that an ex-lover can become a genuine friend, so don't try and make it easier on him by saying that you can still remain buddies. If he still loves you, all you'll be doing is committing him to slow and frustrating torture every time he sees you. He may keep a brave face on it, but *hope* is a crazy and irrational feeling, and lovers are capable of living in hope even when there is none at all.

What happens if he's living in your apartment, and you're not only faced with the problem of telling him it's all over—you have to evict him as well?

How you handle this little cookie depends on the guy. If he's a proud man who knows when to call it a day, then he'll pack up and leave you without any disturbance. Allow him a few days to find somewhere else to live, and even if you're angry with him, don't go throwing his clothes and belongings into the hallway. You respected him once, and the least you can do is give him the oportunity to exit with dignity.

If he steadfastly refuses to leave, saying he still loves you and he won't go, then you may have to take a week's holiday. Tell him you want him out by the time you get back, and that's all there is to it. A word to the wise, though: don't leave anything of value in your apartment when you take that vacation. Absolutely the last thing you want at this moment in time is the sordid complication of accusing your ex-lover of larceny or vandalism.

If he *still* steadfastly refuses to leave, then he has no class at all, and your friendly neighborhood police department may have to assist you in levering him off the premises. Before you blow the whistle, though, you could have a try at a slum landlord's special: throwing out his belongings and changing the lock before he gets home from work. I hope that you never have to face a situation like that, though, and you probably never will if you're *decisive* about ending your relationship right from the moment you first tell him. He will only hang on, after all, if he has some faint glimmering hope that you're going to change your mind. Tough as it seems, you must never give him that hope.

After the chop come the telephone calls and the letters. If he still loves you, he won't give up easily, and you can't expect him to. You'd feel just the same if a man you loved tried to cut you out of his life as well. But again, it's vital that you're firm. Don't agree to see him "just for a quick drink," or "just to talk things over." It's all been said and there's nothing more to discuss. If he writes, be polite enough to write back, but be cool and distant and quite conclusive.

> Dear Jack:
> Thank you for your letter. I appreciate how you feel, and I'm sorry you've been hurt. But my mind is quite made up. I don't want to see you again. I enjoyed it while it lasted, but now it's completely over, and I want to look for new things in life. I hope you'll be happy.
>
> Love,
> Jill.

One thing I haven't made up *my* mind about is what a girlfriend of mine is blunt enough to call The Grand Finale Fuck. She says that whenever she breaks up with a lover, she always gets into bed with him for a last glorious bout of intercourse. "It's better," she says, "than a handshake."

Whether you'll want to get into Grand Finales or not will depend on you, and the stresses in your situation, and just how your lover will take the idea. Another girl I know, when I suggested she give her lovers a Grand Finale, said in amazement: "They'd kick me straight out of the door."

Some Grand Finales, not surprisingly, turn into Grand New Beginnings. Tessa, a 24-year-old Rochester girl, told me the following personal story: "Chris and I were in a real bad way. We hardly talked to each other, and it was pretty obvious that our relationship was going out of the window. But I guess we were both stubborn, and neither of us wanted to be the first to admit that it was a washout, because the *other* one would have turned around and said, 'Oh, so you think it's a washout, do you? Well, *I* don't, but if that's the way you feel—' You know the kind of argument I mean.

"I guess we were drifting apart because we were both heavily into our work. Chris was getting together a huge nationwide consumer survey that was incredibly important to his whole career. If it worked out the way he hoped, it meant almost immediate promotion. And I was into a special seminar for infant-school teachers, and I had so much work on my plate I didn't know where to turn.

"In the last few weeks, we hardly ever made love at all. If we did, we did it silently, because we both had sexual appetites and because we needed to relieve ourselves, but it was about as romantic and as meaningful as brushing your teeth or scratching your armpit.

"One Sunday afternoon, I decided I'd had it. Chris was working on his goddam survey, and he hadn't said a word all day. What was I supposed to do, turn into a silent nun because a certain percentage of United States citizens happen to eat one kind of breakfast cereal and another percentage can't stand the sight of the stuff?

"I went up to Chris and I said, 'That's it.' He said, 'That's what?' I said, 'That's it. It's all over. You and me are washed up. Pick up what's yours and get yourself back home.'

"He still didn't say anything. He collected all his books and his LPs, and he stacked them outside by his car, and he just seemed to accept the situation. I was glad, because I couldn't have stopped myself from crying if he'd tried to argue.

"I was standing in the kitchen when he'd collected everything. He took my hand and said, 'Tessa, there's something I think we ought to do, because we've been together for two years and somehow it won't seem right if we end it any other way.'

"I said, 'What's that?', but I knew what he meant. He said, 'Come to bed. One last time.'

"I was shaking when I went into the bedroom with

him. The drapes were closed, and it was cool and dark in there. Chris stood up straight in front of me, and he took off his clothes. His penis was very high and hard. I kept thinking to myself that this was the last time I'd see it, and the last time I'd feel it. Then he undressed me, taking off my kaftan and my jeans, and my gym shoes. He always laughed when I wore gym shoes, and he smiled then, when he was taking them off. I was checking my tears as much as I could, but I could feel them running down my face in spite of myself. Chris didn't seem to notice. He kissed me on the cheek and his lips were wet with my tears, but he didn't say a word.

"We climbed on to the bed, and he caressed my breasts, and rubbed my nipples between his fingers. They rose up stiff, and he pinched them gently, and gave me all kinds of feelings in my breasts that I'd almost forgotten about. I usually feel very sensitive in my breasts—I mean I get very quickly turned on if somebody caresses them—and even though I was feeling very choky and uptight, the things that Chris was doing were making me feel warm and excited.

"His hands stroked around my body, and around my thighs. And do you know something else, he began to turn me on in a way that he never had done before. It wasn't because he hadn't *tried* before, or because he was lazy about sex or anything, although there had been plenty of times when he could have made more effort. But the reason he was turning me on so much was because I had told him it was all over, and for the first time in two years we didn't have any responsibilities to each other any longer. We could have sex any way we liked, and tomorrow didn't matter, because it was all over anyway.

"He knelt down between my legs, and he dipped his tongue into my cunt. He licked away at me until I could actually feel my clitoris rising up as hard as his penis, and in the end I had to reach down and pull him up on to me, because I needed his penis in my cunt. I held it in my hand, his penis, and it was so hard that I could hardly get my fingers around it. I held it in both hands, and stretched my legs wide open, and brought his penis right up between my legs like one of those people in Shakespeare who are going to stab themselves. And I stabbed myself in the cunt with his big hard penis, and then I reached around and clung on to his hard muscly ass, and I pushed him into me as far as he would go, which was too far, because it hurt, but I wanted the hurt just then.

"We fucked as we always did, in silence, but this silence was different than it had ever been before. We were silent because we were listening for each other's reactions, and whether we were breathing fast or slow. He fucked me with such beautiful style, it was like a kind of exotic dance. Erotic dance, as well. His penis seemed to glide in and out me at all kinds of complicated angles and stimulate me in all kinds of different ways. It wasn't all that long before I realized I was higher than I'd ever been on sex, and everything that was happening was like a dream.

"I don't know why he did what he did at the end, but somehow it was the right thing. Just as he was going to climax, he took his penis out of me, and he held it in his hand, and right in front of me he spouted out all his white semen, all over the sheets of the bed. Perhaps he wanted to make his mark on the bed, or something. Perhaps he just wanted to show me how he came. I actually watched it pouring out of the end of his penis, and it seemed to come in slow motion, and glide through the air in streams.

"I went face down on the bed and I licked his semen up from the bed. I knew then that I didn't want any souvenirs, or any marks, but I wanted him. I was having a strange kind of orgasm all the time this was happening, it was like a kind of physical earthquake that started off with little trembles, and by the time I was crawling around the bed, licking up his semen, I was gasping and shaking, and my legs were stiff and convulsed.

"We both lay in the dark for a long time. Then I said, 'Chris?' and he said, 'What?' and I said, 'Stay. Make it like this all the time, and stay.' And he said, 'Okay, I will.' And that was all.

"Sometimes it's as good as that 'last time,' and sometimes it's not, but on that day we got scared of losing each other, and we realized just how much we were capable of loving each other if we tried, and so these days we try harder."

Don't expect a magic answer to your relationship's problems from the Grand Finale Fuck, however. The reason it occasionally works is *because* neither of you are expecting anything out of it. Do it if you want to, but don't think that fireworks will fill the sky, surf will thunder over the beach, and Rhett Butler will appear over the horizon. More often than not, Grand Finale Fucks end up with one lover or the other being more dissatisfied than ever before. I know—I've done one myself.

Give yourself a little time to get over the lover you've lost, or the lover you've jilted. Go to parties and visit friends, and be sociable and jolly, but also allow yourself a limited amount of good old-fashioned moping. It's part of the whole process of healing your wounds, that lonesome walk in the park on a wintry afternoon, with your tears splashing into the icy lake.

When you find another man (which you inevitably will, because you've read this book, and when you've read this book, you'll know how to please *anyone*), don't try and burden him too much with the sorrows of your past relationship. He will be interested to know something about it, because it will tell him something about you and your personality, and he will also be able to understand that you're capable of deep and lasting love.

But don't go on and *on* about Mr. Previous Lover, because that will begin to grate on his nerves, and he'll begin to wonder if you're still carrying a torch for him. Men like to appear tolerant and understanding about their sexual predecessors, but most of the time they're very jealous and suspicious. They'll deny it—but I'm a man, and I know damn well they are.

Another word to the wise: don't slander your previous

flame to the new man in your life. He may half-enjoy hearing that his precursor had a smaller cock, wasn't half so well educated, so confident, so loving or good-looking, but it will serve your relationship better if you tell your new man the truth. Tell him that you did love his predecessor, that he was okay, but that things just didn't work out.

Because if you don't show that you're loyal to the man you left behind, your new lover is going to start wondering what you'll say about *him* to the next in line. Telling a man about your previous sad good-bye is no way to say a happy new hallo. *Comprende?*

# 27.

## *The Erotically Perfect Pair*

"I'm well read in women, I seldom can find
One that brings a new relish of joy to my mind;
But she's quite a treat, one that never can pall,
Think all you can think, she surpasses it all."
      —"Epistle to a Lady," anonymous, ca. 1890

No book about sex can ever cover every contingency and every eventuality that you may come across in your erotic relationships. In some ways, it is presumptuous to call this book a guide to tell you how to drive your man wild in bed, because as we have seen from the women who have contributed their views on sex, a great deal of your success will depend on the response you get from your lover.

That's why, in fact, this book was written as one of a

pair. The other—*How To Be The Perfect Lover\**—looks at the same problems from the man's point of view, and if you and your lover or husband were each to read the appropriate book, you'd both have a fairly well-rounded view of what a constructive and mutually satisfying sex life can be.

Despite the fact that so much depends on *who* you make love with, I still believe that facts, information, suggestions, training and technique are essential parts of any woman's grounding in sex. It's not enough to know how babies are made, and why you bleed every month, and what men's penises look like. It's not even enough to know intercourse positions, and what to do on your wedding night.

In a society that places so much emphasis on sex and sex behavior, books for women that tell them exactly what men are going to expect of them—and what they can expect from men—are scandalously rare. Those sex books which have been specifically aimed at women— like *The Sensuous Woman*—almost always restrict themselves to a candyfloss idea of a bedtime nirvana with a man who's always sexually rampant, always obliging, and always in a good humor. As we've seen, men are certainly not always like that.

If you've read this book carefully, and tried to follow its training instructions to the best of your ability, your knowledge about sex, both straightforward and kinky, will be as good, if not better, than that of any man you're likely to meet. I'm not suggesting you should tell him that in so many words, because men are notoriously sensitive about their sexual knowledge, but at least very few things that any man is likely to do to you or want *you* to do to him will now take you by surprise.

You will be the perfect lover to the extent that you will be able to cope with and understand any sexual demand that your lovers will make, and be able to distinguish between the light-hearted love game and the not-so-frolicsome perversion. I hope that as time goes by

* *How To Be The Perfect Lover*, Signet Books, 1975.

I'll receive fewer letters that say things like "My husband wants me to pee on him—is this all right?" or "My lover likes smearing me with raspberry jam and rolling on top of me—is this normal?"

There's one further thing I want to say about the responsibilities of a sexually sophisticated woman, and that's about contraception. I've saved this until last because I believe it's one of the most serious and important aspects of any sexual relationship you have with a man.

Although, in *The Perfect Lover*, I have made it clear to men that it is *their* responsibility to ensure that you don't become pregnant, it is still not enough to rely on a man's discretion. After all, he might not have read the book. If you're *likely* to be having sexual relationships with men, have your doctor prescribe a contraceptive pill for you. Don't wait until the sexual relationship has started, because you can make a baby just as easily the first time as you can on the 99th time.

If, for any physiologic reason, you're not suited to a contraceptive pill, then you can have a coil fitted. This is a contraceptive device that is inserted into the uterus by a specialist. Sex researchers are not entirely clear how it works, but it does.

Failing those methods, fit yourself up with a diaphragm, which is a dome of rubber, with a springy circular base, which fits over the neck of your womb and prevents sperm from entering. A diaphragm should always be used in conjunction with a spermicidal cream or jelly.

If you're without any of the above, then always keep a condom or two handy in your purse. They're cheap, they're effective, and they fit any man alive (with the possible exception of the guy in East Africa I was telling you about) . Don't ever rely on a guy to have his own.

Contraceptive methods that don't work, or may be dangerous: the infamous *withdrawal method*, in which the man takes his penis out of you just before he's about to ejaculate. What many users of this method don't appreciate is that (a) sperms can escape from the penis *be-*

*fore* ejaculation proper, and that (b) even the tiniest drop of sperm on the lips of the vagina can lead to impregnation. What's more, if used regularly, this method can be very frustrating for both of you.

Then there's *contraceptive film,* which is a small patch of spermicidal material placed inside your vagina or on the end of his penis. Recent tests have shown that an unacceptably high number of women have become pregnant through using this method alone, and the manufacturers have had to add instructions that film must be used in conjunction with other contraceptive methods.

*American tips,* as they're sometimes called, are small condoms which fit over the head of the penis alone, and are secured around the corona. If they stay on, you're reasonably safe, but they have a nasty habit of slipping off, and then you're definitely not safe.

The *rhythm method.* Approved by the Roman Catholic Church, this method involves having sex only on certain days of the month, in between a woman's period and her next ovulation. I don't want to get into any religious or ethical arguments about this method, but I can only say that statistics indisputably show that users of this method bear more children than users of other methods.

What does a woman do if she becomes pregnant?

The answer depends greatly on the circumstances. The responsibility is as much yours as it is his, and as much his as it is yours. If you do become pregnant, no matter how concerned you are about what it may do to your relationship, you must tell him. If you both decide you want to get rid of the baby through an abortion, then he should pay you at least half the cost. He's not legally bound to, of course, and there's no way in which you can force him, but if he's worth knowing at all, that's what he'll do.

If he wants you to keep it and you don't want to, you'll have to make a choice. It's your body that has to go through nine months of labor, and you that will have to look after a child through at least 16 years of growing-up, so the decision is certainly yours. But you may lose your lover through anger or resentment, and you'll have to work out for yourself how he's going to take it. The same applies if you want to keep the child and he doesn't want to know.

If you do decide to have the baby, then have a long think about the baby itself. Don't think about it as a cuddly little newborn child, but as a five-year-old, as a ten-year-old, as a man or a woman, having to cope with all the problems that illegitimate birth can bring it. It's not easy, being a bastard.

The only other word I can say about contraception is: *do*.

Now that you're ready to go out and drive your man wild in bed, there's one other thing you can do that will help you to build a creative sex life. You may do it already—in which case, you're armed with an important aid to your own sexual development.

Keep a diary (locked, of course) in which you write down as detailed an account as possible of what happens to you in your sexual relationships with men. Despite the intensity of sex, it's surprising how quickly you forget what you actually did and what you actually felt, and to be able to look back on your experiences and your mistakes is very valuable to you.

What's more, it's something you'll be able to look back on with more than a touch of nostalgia when you're 83, and rocking in your Grand Rapids chair in front of the fire.

"Those," you can say, "were the days when I really drove them wild."

Thank you for reading. Lots of love—and good luck.

Graham Masterton has worked on publications dealing with sexual topics for eight years. He edited *Penthouse, Mayfair, Forum,* and the Swedish pornography magazine *Private.* He has also written six books on sexual behavior. Mr. Masterton, who collects nineteenth-century porcelain and is a deadly accurate pistol shot, is twenty-nine years old and lives in Epsom Downs, England.